I enthusiastically endorse Doug's vision—especially his dedicated focus on a collaborative approach to strategic planning. This book embodies Doug's professionalism and perfectionism, which I observed firsthand while working with him for over a decade: he is the rare engineer who is totally immersed in the business of consulting, and his unparalleled strategic prowess is undeniably reflected in these pages.

—Al Curran, PE, co-founder and former CEO and Chairman, Woodard & Curran

Al Curran and Frank Woodard founded Woodard & Curran in 1979. Al was CEO for over 25 years

Doug's in-the-trenches leadership experience shines through in this well-organized text. Doug clearly understands that well-meaning strategies can only be realized with thoughtful preparation for and commitment to barrier-busting support. Doug's unique career path has enabled him to intimately connect to a broad range of employees who can and should be engaged to advance the firm.

—Fred Kramer, AIA, Vice President, Northeast Buildings Division, Stantec

Fred was CEO of the 250 person Architecture firm ADD Inc. which merged with Stantec in 2014

If you're an executive who wants to lead business growth effectively, look no further than Doug Reed. Doug is an expert in teaching how to effect change by positively influencing elements that you don't directly control. With an abundance of proficient practical analysis and actionable advice, Doug's book will give you the roadmap for wrestling effectively with the dynamics of any marketplace to grow your business.

—Bill Marrazzo, President/CEO of WHYY

Prior to WHYY Philadelphia, Bill was President and CEO of Weston Solutions and Commissioner of Philadelphia Water. Bill has served on many corporate boards

A rare and refreshing work that is chock-full of insight from someone who "gets it." Doug builds on tried-and-true strategic planning methods while adding his own to synthesize a unique methodology perfectly suited to the 21st century A/E industry.

Doug's proven experience in identifying and overcoming A/E business barriers, and his interactive teaching approach has been invaluable to our own strategic planning process. Doug continues to coach our staff and has become a valued partner to our management team.

—Chris Mulleavey, PE, President/CEO, Hoyle, Tanner & Associates, Inc.

LEAD

A

MOVEMENT

LEAD

— A —

MOVEMENT

THE INSIDER'S GUIDE TO
POWERFUL STRATEGY EXECUTION

DOUGLAS F. REED

Printed in the United States of America

Paperback ISBN: 978-949639-00-1
eBook ISBN: 978-1-949639-03-2

Library of Congress Number: 2018954362

Rev. 1

TABLE OF CONTENTS

CHAPTER 1

WE TRIED THIS ALREADY. IT DIDN'T WORK

If you think back thirty, forty, or more years, do you remember the kind of emotional high you had when you led the football or debate team through a challenging season, all the way to the title? Or how about the moment that letter of acceptance came from the university you'd spent years preparing to attend?

The feeling that comes from hard-won success is hard to beat—and hard to replicate on a daily basis. Its opposite, the sting of failure (or perceived failure), is hard to live with—when your final year of high school basketball was a losing season no matter how hard you played; or you weren't accepted into the grad school of your choice; or you didn't get the girl, the boy, or the job you wanted. Negative experiences like that can leave indelible marks—unless your attention is focused on the value of learned lessons and the opportunity they provide to advance.

Feelings of failure can be insidious. The experience of *losing face* can be paralyzing. Perhaps this has happened to you. Unresolved failure can impede future success. The most common unresolved business failure is a good strategy never executed.

The lessons and case studies described in this book are relevant to any service business, but they are of particular value to senior managers, principals, and C-suite executives in architecture, engineering, environmental, and construction management firms. If you influence the direction and success of your company, or aspire to hold such a position in the future, this book is for you.

Lead a Movement will reveal how you can successfully execute strategy. The methodology has been perfected over my thirty-plus years of aiding firms with strategic growth and finding practical solutions where others couldn't. We will explore the reasons why efforts to execute strategies can fail. We will learn how to cultivate leadership based upon putting forth a vision and building a movement. We will also come to understand why it is imperative for a business to continue to grow at all times. "Grow" does not have to mean "bigger." But it does mean that evolution must occur. The stakes could not be higher: failing to properly plan or execute strategy could derail a massive, years-long project. It could spell the end of your job (if not your career). In the worst case, it could jeopardize the health of the entire firm.

I've spent years partnering with architectural, engineering, and environmental firms to develop and execute *safe growth* strategies. If your business has difficulty reaching financial goals, expanding into new services or markets, rolling out initiatives that gain traction, or retaining quality employees, it may be time to reconsider your approach. My goal for your business is strategy execution that produces growth with certainty, not chance. Safe, yet robust growth along with enviable profitability that compromises neither vision nor integrity—and in fact enhances both.

But first, while growth may seem like a simple concept, it's actually somewhat complicated. So exactly how do we define growth when it comes to your business?

DEFINING GROWTH

For the purposes of this book, I have broken growth down into six categories:

- Wealth

- Acquisition

- Key hires

- Organic

- High profile

- Geographic

WEALTH AND GROWTH

When companies talk about growth at the C-suite level, they're typically talking about growing wealth, or increasing their revenue and profit. For owners, growth in wealth manifests itself in increased stock value. The growth of wealth and profit can also benefit employees who are partial owners. Though they may own just a very small percentage of the company, wealth and profit contribute to their financial well-being.

Growing wealth can also be part of a game plan to sell the company. Steps must be taken to increase the purchase price when the company is offered, which puts the focus on a term used often in the acquisitions arena: EBITDA, or Earnings Before Income, Taxes, Depreciation, and Amortization. But what happens when strategies for increasing revenue and wealth don't work?

Ride the Great Unknown to Wealth?

A group of investors formed a partnership to take advantage of growing social concerns about the environment and sustainability. They began buying environmental services firms, and after a few years they had accumulated five firms in various parts of the country. They hired a former banker and CPA to manage the combined firms part-time, retained the office managers for each of the purchased firms, and waited for the industry to grow.

Ten years later, the industry had expanded substantially. But the combined performance of their firms did not deliver the expected return on investment. The firms' services had degraded into commodity services, driving margins down due to extreme customer price sensitivity.

Luckily for them, a large, oil industry–related environmental disaster occurred near one of their locations, and business exploded for that location. Revenue soared. The investors quickly spun off this unit for a profit and continued to manage the remaining four locations.

The investors had no experience in the environmental services industry, but they recognized that it was destined to grow. So the plan was to rely on the employees, who knew the business. The CPA-turned-CEO was also unfamiliar with the industry, so he turned to industry experts to help with sales. None were able to improve the bottom line. There were several attempts to attract a buyer, but none of the offers they received were financially attractive. Years passed, and frustration grew.

Finally, the CPA hired an industry business consultant, who coached management in each location to help them learn to target more profitable clients, and who advised the investors to take over another firm in another location. The consultant then helped the investors to realize that the office managers did not have the business skills to grow their units. Accomplishing that would have required additional hiring to execute a much more aggressive marketing and sales program. At this point, the investors' patience had worn thin. Revenue and profit were way off. They directed the CPA to find a buyer at any price, and he did.

In this example, the investors did not lose money, but neither did they make money. There are many lessons from this story that will be explored later in the book. In such a business investment plan, there are many red flags: no direct experience in the industry; relying on office managers who were proficient in operations, not growth; a CPA who lacked business growth skills and personnel management skills; and a plan that left the investment vulnerable to market forces. A lucky event—the disaster—had made it possible for one investment to pay off, but should a business strategy depend on luck? Is there a way to develop an investment strategy based on certainty? Yes, there is, and this book will demonstrate how to plan and support such an effort so that everyone, from top-level leadership down to low-level staff, can contribute.

GROWTH BY ACQUISITION

Acquiring other companies is another way some firms seek to expand their footprint. Sometimes called "bolt-ons," acquisitions facilitate ventures into new services, new client markets, and new geographical areas. But like most things, acquiring other firms needs to be done with a well-designed and executed game plan. The firm or firms under consideration must be thoroughly vetted. The acquiring firm has to have staff and processes to support the instant expansion. An acquisition may unknowingly be undertaken in reaction to flaws at home. Here's what can happen when an acquisition strategy fails:

Acquisitions from Hell

The CEO of a midsize architectural/engineering firm was intent on creating shareholder value. This CEO had previously been COO, and had assumed his role during a major recession; the firm was now barely half its former size. Fortunately, it still had two of its three offices.

Though the economy was recovering, business was not increasing fast enough to restore the firm to its former size any time soon. The CEO retained an external advisor to formulate a strategic plan, and this advisor charted a path to regain the company's strength and move into the emerging energy market. The firm immediately acted to acquire firms in adjacent locations. Over five years, four firms were acquired that leveraged geographies for the original firm's core transportation and environmental services. A fifth was acquired that also brought with it a team focused on energy services.

At first, each office was welcomed with open arms. New staff were introduced through multiple meetings and retreats. Each firm's administrative services were integrated into the parent firm over the first year. But sales did not grow. Profitability for those firms remained elusive.

At four of the firms, the owners were planning on retiring. While they stayed on for several years, their motivation was low, and they spent most of their time in their retirement destinations. Adding to the challenge, key people and midlevel staff departed these firms, leaving behind about half the original staff. No one wanted to lead sales or corporate management efforts.

At the fifth firm, an owner with his eye on the exit did remain and transitioned to sales, but things suffered. The firm's core business had declined, and the owner—now in sales—had moved into a new market. He continued to sell in that new market, but lacked the strong skills needed for real success, having spent his previous forty years working in another capacity.

Nevertheless, the parent company's CEO was committed to making it all work, no matter what. He personally took on the task of growing the new acquisitions. He enlisted quite a few of his principals to share the effort, but it seemed they never had the time for it. Consequently, he was going it alone. He spent long days traveling throughout the region of the country where the acquired firms were located, staying in hotels while he attempted to support sales and project delivery. At best, he was in each office one day a week.

He soon came to realize that most of the offices had senior staff who were poor project managers and were not able to expand sales beyond a handful of loyal clients. He had to fire several, but he had no replacements.

Then it really hit the fan. The last acquisition was performing abysmally. Its main problem was a poor delivery system, particularly poor quality control. The CEO learned that many clients were unhappy, even angry. And regulators involved with some of the projects had come to think of that firm in a negative light.

Soon the CEO was spending three out of five days doing damage control for that one acquisition. He brought in staff resources from headquarters to help, but they were working with no budget to fix problem projects. The financials grew worse. In fact, everything got worse. Several clients served notice that they intended to sue if project problems—including construction claims associated with errors and omissions—could not be resolved. The CEO went into overdrive trying to resolve the claims.

Now the CEO had no time for the two smallest of the five acquisitions, which also were in the most remote locations. He made the difficult decision to shut them down, laying off staff members who had not already left.

Without much support from the parent firm's five senior principals, who were busy with local projects, the CEO decided he had to settle all claims and move on. Over the course of a year, he negotiated settlements and drew on the insurance policies of the acquired companies until the policy limits were reached. Luckily, this coverage was available because the project problems had begun prior to the acquisition. Still, it was no fun to pay off all those claims.

With his reputation in tatters, debts high, and net profits negative, the CEO decided after his ten-year tenure that it was time to step down. Later, he confided to me, "I failed as a CEO. I should have stuck to my COO role."

This unfortunate story does have an encouraging epilogue. I was brought in by the CEO as a turnaround specialist, and within three years the company enjoyed profits in the top 20 percent tier of the industry. Eventually it returned to its peak number of employees. And all this was accomplished without any acquisitions. Growth through acquisition is a powerful strategy, but one that presents many pitfalls if not done right. This book will enable you to avoid succumbing to the same strategic errors.

GROWTH THROUGH KEY HIRES

Many companies attempt to achieve growth with a **key hire**—someone with a special ability such as technical or sales prowess who will increase profitability. Like acquisitions, key hires may be intended to move a business into markets it does not currently service.

My experience with key hires is that while some may achieve the goals for which they are tapped, more often than not the company sees the new hire as a white knight—a savior. It's a fantasy, something that in literature is called a *deus ex machina*: the god who comes down from the heavens at the last minute to save the day. But they don't always work. The following is a prime example.

All Hail! Our Savior Has Arrived!

A large engineering and environmental services firm was compelled to complete a new strategic plan because one of its core markets had matured and demand was drying up. Two options were identified: one was to invest in a core service area to grow it into a major part of the company's business. The other was to enter a new market for the declining set of services.

Two key hires were made. One was a seasoned veteran who had worked on the client side of the new market. The other was a widely known and respected industry expert. A time frame of two years was established to integrate these new hires and show substantial new bookings. The CEO and practice leaders of the two service areas were excited to have this support.

The effort required considerable travel: flights, hotels, conferences, and many meetings with the contacts known to the two key hires. Flash-forward a year: the seasoned veteran had racked up more than a dozen conferences and fifty meetings, many over expensive lunches or dinners, without much impact. Nearly half of these required the attendance of headquarters staff.

Sales meetings were frequent, at least one every two weeks. Lists of prospects were reviewed, and a pattern emerged. The seasoned veteran easily scored meetings with people he knew, but only rarely could he get an audience with someone he didn't know. And many of those he knew were not key decision makers—they were midlevel employees, just as he had been. They were friends.

Every once in a while he learned of an RFP from his friends' organizations. But there was always an incumbent, and it became apparent that most of the time incumbents were retained directly, so there was no chance to submit. The few RFPs that did come their way ended up as lost pursuits because cost, not relationships or qualifications, trumped other criteria.

The seasoned veteran grew frustrated, as did his employer's management team. One day he gave notice. He was going to a position in his industry similar to the one he'd held before.

The other key hire, the industry expert, was named a practice leader. In this position he was expected to lead sales and mentor staff. He was soon in great demand internally to support projects. However, despite his status as an expert, it soon became apparent that he had little time for sales. And while the firm had the ability to deliver an array of services to that market, this person preferred to stick to topics in which he was already well versed.

It was decided he needed to train junior staff to take on his workload to free him up for sales. Over two years, several staff members attempted to work with him, but they complained that he was too busy to get them involved. He was a poor delegator and wanted to keep the work to himself.

Two years later, the only new business related to this expert had been won by others. The number of pursuits he'd led could be counted on one hand. The overall revenue and profitability of the practice remained static, which meant that staff size remained the same.

In reality, a single individual alone can't turn around a struggling firm. Without the support of the right people and the right processes, they will fail. This book will show how to integrate new hires within an overarching strategy in a way that packs a powerful punch.

ORGANIC GROWTH

Sometimes growth is tied to internal factors such as achieving sales excellence and improving a firm's employee recruiting and retention rate. This is considered **organic** growth in contrast to an acquisition growth strategy. This strategy requires a focus on career advancement so that competent, ambitious staff members don't have to look elsewhere. These employees often think of growth in terms of the trajectory of their careers. Exposure to new technical challenges and a stimulating work environment in which employees can learn from superiors and peers are key factors in individual growth. Often these are the core drivers behind the kind of growth employees really want. And for a business, it's just as important to spend time focusing on people's individual goals as it is to increase revenue and profits.

Succession planning can also be a key component of organic growth, and it must be handled meticulously. Done right, it's your company's ticket to longevity. Done wrong, as this next example illustrates, it's the beginning of the end.

Who's Next?

The engineering and planning firm was one of the oldest in a large city. Several generations of leadership had come and gone. The firm operated in markets where price competition was common, as were overhead and profit controls. Its operation was lean, and costs were tightly controlled. Utilization was by far the number one key performance metric.

The CEO and CFO were about the same age, and they had decided to exit the same year. They'd built a management team with a familiar three-legged stool approach: the third leg was a bright MBA who was a few years younger and had been with the firm for more than twenty years.

The three worked together well and made almost all of the decisions. They had a formal management team who mostly concerned themselves with staffing and, to a lesser degree, sales.

Eventually the elder principals retired and joined the firm's board as advisors. A new CEO embarked on a strategic planning effort with two key concerns. First, the company had shrunk by more than 50 percent in the Great Recession and was now only marginally profitable. Second, the new CEO wanted to exit in four years.

Immediately after completing the strategic plan, the firm's twenty-five principals were energized. They were going to become great at hiring valuable employees. They were going to improve processes, particularly project management and sales. And they were going to work on a successor.

Now the three-legged stool structure no longer existed. The CEO had a new CFO, but he underperformed. There was a process-focused principal, but he was not popular, and in particular was not compatible with the CEO. Another well-liked and effective principal was located in a remote office, and largely managed that division independent of headquarters, even though there were units in both offices delivering the same services.

The CEO was reluctant to engage too many people in executing the strategic plan, so he chose a couple of simple elements of the plan and took them on himself. Progress stalled, and those involved with the strategic planning, knowing the CEO's exit was imminent, began to leave the firm.

The CEO's announced retirement date was now just one year away, and no replacement candidates had been identified. An executive recruiter was retained. Six months later, in a hot economy, one of the senior principals was recruited away. Still, no satisfactory CEO candidates had surfaced. There were two pretty good candidates, but they withdrew themselves from consideration after receiving an unsatisfactory answer when they asked why the firm had no internal successor. The answer given was that no one was qualified or interested. This concerned them, as it revealed that no one had been given real leadership responsibilities. Good candidates would walk away after realizing that the company had no effective leaders.

The CEO kept postponing his retirement. By now he was three years past retirement age, and his wife was very unhappy that they were unable to visit their faraway grandchildren. But the CEO did not want to leave his staff high and dry.

Ultimately, the CEO despaired of attracting an acceptable candidate to the firm. He reluctantly hired a business broker, and the firm was sold to a massive conglomerate that had gobbled up many local firms in the industry. The firm's inability to hire meant they could not increase revenue. The price was attractive for the buyer, but shareholders only received a modest return on their investments.

Epilogue: the new owner was familiar with neither the local market nor the firm's services. Most of the senior principals left. The

CEO retired, and although he enjoyed spending time with grand-children, he always felt guilty for not growing leadership organically or allowing anyone to step up and be his partner in managing the business. Later in the book, we'll look more closely at how organic growth fits into an organization-wide strategy that stimulates the development of homegrown leadership and fully taps into a firm's talent.

HIGH-PROFILE GROWTH

Some years back, I was retained by an architectural firm whose growth strategy was to enhance its global reputation. The principals were courting fame in order to become involved with more note-worthy international projects. Their path to organic growth was retaining quality employees who'd be stimulated and motivated by the caliber of clients the firm would represent. They were not inter-ested in getting bigger, just more famous by escalating the profile of the work they delivered.

This high-profile approach was tricky as it required that all employees be satisfied with this goal for their own career. The challenge was to make sure there was a defined career path for these employees—especially the junior members of the organization. The company had to be positioned to burnish its reputation while providing employees with clear advancement opportunities timed with the retirement of senior principals. If a well-executed plan is not in place, despite the kind of clients a firm may attract, ambitious employees will have no choice but to go elsewhere. Fortunately for this firm, we were able to implement changes in the organizational structure that ensured highly competent employees always had a home where they felt valued and were able to grow professionally by taking on ever more complex or creative work.

GEOGRAPHICAL GROWTH

Sometimes a company's blueprint for growth may hinge on geography. The firm may believe that expansion into a new territory or territories is the cure for straggling revenue. But do the leaders have a calculated strategy for expanding the firm in that way?

The Wagon Train to Greener Pastures

Some believe that if you can't achieve profitable growth locally, you should go where there is more promise. But although the grass may look greener elsewhere, there is opportunity right under your nose if you know how to find it.

A fifty-year-old mechanical, electrical, and plumbing engineering (MEP) firm had plodded along with twenty-five employees for twenty years. Then a third-generation CEO with a business background took over—a CEO who knew how to sell and how to empower staff to do so. The firm exploded to 250 employees and multiple offices. The fourth-generation CEO was different: a technical person by nature who believed that tight controls were the best approach to growth.

Ten years later, the firm had weathered two recessions, but only barely. It had shrunk to under 120 employees—twice.

After the pain of layoffs from the first recession, the recovery had brought back growth. This was an opportunity, or so the CEO thought, to expand to other locations that were likely to enjoy more sustained growth, and might even be immune to recession. The firm began by submitting new proposals in a targeted state, and learned that teaming with a local firm was important. Management identified a potential partner, and it so happened that the owner was near retirement and was interested in selling the firm, so the firm purchased it.

The CEO was overjoyed. There was now a new office in the new location. Economic forecasts projected strong growth there. Clients had massive infrastructure expansion plans, and the state government was moving full speed ahead to position the state as an economic powerhouse.

Now the flashback: I met several members of the MEP firm's management team at a local professional association meeting. The MEP services were complemented by civil engineering and architecture pursuits. Since I was a principal in an A/E firm, I sensed a business teaming opportunity. I suggested we have our management teams meet to explore beginning a long-term teaming relationship.

All ten principals attended the meeting except for the other firm's CEO. In our conference room with my own team of principals, we shared firm history, experience, and growth plans. The other team volunteered that they had just started a venture in a high-growth region through an acquisition. I asked them how the acquisition was going.

The first person gave it a positive review. They had secured business there and were working on shared projects. The next person acknowledged this and mentioned that long-distance management was challenging. The following person sighed and related that the effort was much more difficult than they had expected. Then the next principal admitted that there were many surprises—things they'd learned about the firm *after the acquisition.*

Suddenly, the honesty valve was thrown wide open. The principals all said that the experience had become the most miserable of their careers. The reputation of the acquired firm was, contrary to their expectations, bad. It was limited by weak processes, inconsistent performance, and unpopular (and sometimes indifferent) leadership.

Instead of focusing on their home territory to protect their gains, they were lavishing excessive attention on the new territory. To make matters worse, while that state had been a national model for rapid economic growth, the ongoing recession was shattering the new economy. Private sector clients applied the brakes. Industry peers were laying off staff and closing offices. In fact, the economic downturn had hit that state far harder than the region where the company was headquartered.

There are many lessons evident in this debacle. Were the firm's own processes ready to handle the sudden increase in company size? Probably not. Was there any single person at headquarters who was passionate enough to take on the acquisition? No. Did the principals of the firm first become familiar enough with the new territory to learn about the hidden reputation issues? Apparently not. The firm's "wagon train" was not well designed and adequately provisioned.

As I said at the beginning of the chapter, when growth strategies fail, the sting of failure can cause a kind of company paralysis that hampers growth. We don't want to look bad, feel bad, suffer more loss, or "go through that again." After the horse has thrown us and we've gotten hurt, it's hard to get back on and ride. Though most companies adopt a "move on" mindset after such events, the fact is if you ask someone about the time things went wrong, their stories may be as clear and potent as if they'd happened yesterday.

So how do we change all that? How do we channel failure into company longevity and the kind of success that comes from growth—*safe growth*?

I'll talk more about safe growth strategies later, but first, we'll take a look at what happens when the choice is made not to grow.

CHAPTER 2

THE BRUTAL TRUTH: GROW OR DIE

Every business owner wants his or her business to grow, right? Actually, the truth is that many don't. And I may be talking about you.

Perhaps they're afraid of losing the company culture. They'll say, "We like the size we are. We're not concerned about growing. We prefer to focus on maintaining our level of expertise. We don't want to go heavy on the business side of things."

At a national conference of professional services firms I attend each year, the focus is on business management. A CEO roundtable is conducted to discuss hot topics. The moderator creates a flip chart to record key topics and the participants vote on the most popular topics. Growth is almost always one of them.

The moderator once began the discussion by saying, "Of course everybody wants to grow." Several people raised their hands, and when the moderator acknowledged them, they informed him that their firms did not choose growth at all. They were content with the way things were. They had zero interest in growing, and that was that.

Taking it one step further, the moderator asked for a show of hands from other CEOs in the group who were not interested in growing their firms. Quite a few hands went up. It was clear that contrary to what you hear in numerous conference presentations, articles, and books, not everyone considers growth a priority.

Does this attitude have negative consequences? Definitely. This mindset of contentment lulls executives into a dangerous state of complacency, as the following true story demonstrates.

WHY GOOD ENOUGH ISN'T

Jim was a project engineer who lived a few miles from work. En route to his office, he encountered several stop signs. At first, he was diligent and stopped fully at each one. Then one day those stops became rolling stops. After all, Jim thought, there really are no consequences of a harmless rolling stop, particularly if one is careful to look left and then right before moving on.

One morning, he was aggravated. He had an argument with his son that caused him to leave for work late. As he drove to the office in an agitated state, one of those rolling stops became more "rolling" than "stop." He did not look carefully left and right before proceeding into the intersection, and bang, he was T-boned.

The other car careened across the intersection and into a fence. Jim jumped out of his car to check on the other driver. She seemed okay save for a burn on her forehead from the airbag. But her car was totaled. She was taken by ambulance to a hospital as a precaution.

Jim didn't hear much more about it after that. His insurance company paid for the damages. He was given a ticket, but it was just a loss of a few dollars. No real harm was done except for a short delay getting to work.

Nevertheless, a month later, he reflected on his habit of rolling through stop signs and how his cavalier attitude about traffic regulations and safe driving had caused problems for him and for somebody else. While it hadn't been a catastrophe, what if something terrible had happened? What if that person had been horribly injured? Why, Jim thought, "I might be in jail!"

This story illustrates the danger of the "We don't want to grow" attitude. For a while, everything seems fine, but eventually the day will come when a slip-up will ruin you. Jim had been cruising along in the Good Enough Zone, and his complacency had made him vulnerable to disaster. If we get stuck in the Good Enough Zone, one day our luck will run out and we will slip.

Avoiding failure requires continuous learning and improvement. This means creating a learning culture. Convey to your team that the Good Enough Zone is dangerous. Instead, you should be forever striving toward excellence.

In his book *Blue Threat*, Tony Kern describes the Good Enough Zone using a stairway metaphor.[1] Envision a stairway that transects three floors. The bottom floor is the failure zone, and the top floor is peak performance. This staircase crosses a middle floor, labeled the Good Enough Zone.

The Good Enough Zone deludes you into believing you're doing well even though you have not grown in terms of revenue or

---

1   Tony Kern, *Blue Threat: Why to Err Is Inhuman* (Pygmy Books, 2009).

profit, number of employees, reputation, or diversification of services offered. You've just kept going the way you are. You're not interested in the world around you—a world that's changing daily. You're not paying attention to risk and vulnerabilities, which can include key employee departures, key clients leaving, and changing performance standards.

Kern stresses that it is critical to pay attention both to what you can control and what you cannot control. As a former Air Force commander, he knew that sometimes we are our own worst enemy. Our own mistakes and oversights can derail the mission as much as our adversary's actions. And that is exactly what happened to Jim.

This means your own complacency and carelessness can doom you. Merely remaining content is tantamount to backsliding, because while you are static everyone else races past you in the pursuit of excellence. The key to sustainability is momentum. The important thing is to always be climbing the stairs, even if slowly.

Always be seeking to improve. Your survival depends on your *willingness* to grow—and your *knowledge* of how to do it safely.

IMPRISONED IN THE STOCKS

What are some of the consequences of not growing?

No growth in the traditional sense means you're not enhancing your profitability, which creates financial hardships because your stock doesn't go up. There is no market for it.

If stock value doesn't increase, there's no internal demand for the stock: it makes distributing ownership among employees problematic. The benefit of distributing ownership is that you're doing some advance planning for internal succession and for current owners. A privately owned firm needs to transfer stock to others, usually incrementally. But no growth in stock deters people from investing in the company. Many companies then end up heavily subsidizing the stock price purchase—which diverts some of their profits into those subsidies. For owners, this has a cost, and if there still isn't a sufficient rate of return from the employees' viewpoint—employees who would be buying the stock—then it's not a long-term, sustainable solution.

What's more, owner retirement can come into play. If one or more owners want to retire or move into other careers, and the staff isn't motivated and ambitious, the owners have no one who can take over the management of the company. At that point the only solution is to dissolve the company or to sell it. Selling it might provide an owner with an exit strategy, but it often leads to instability and other problems for the remaining employees.

It's very difficult to have a succession plan in a company that has a poor track record of growth, and if selling is the goal, the price a buyer is willing to pay is based on profitability and specific growth trends. If the company is flatlining, the sale price is going to be much lower than it should be.

GOING, GOING, GONE

Another consequence of anemic revenue growth is that these firms tend to have high turnover because they do not provide opportunities for advancement. Your product is your people, and you must keep them. If every employee is hoping to advance, and the company is not growing, promotion can only happen when someone leaves or retires. But if there is high turnover, that brings its own set of problems. If too many people are departing, it is hard to maintain consistent performance on client deliverables. It also forces some staff members to allocate an inordinate amount of time to the hiring process. Moreover, each time a new hire comes in, there's a possibility he or she may not work out, which generates even more overhead costs. The ripple effect of growth stagnation is a business staffed with unmotivated, mediocre employees. There are exceptions, but as a rule, those who remain tend to be underperforming individuals who lack drive and ambition.

For the record, I am not talking about the work-life balance that has become increasingly important to millennials and many other highly qualified professionals. I'm talking about employees who may be stuck in the Good Enough Zone. They are not keeping up with new technologies, participating in training, pitching ideas, or generally improving themselves and their value to the company—and hence they are not contributing to the company's value overall. They tend to be comfortable simply sitting back and having assignments handed to them by a few principals.

In all fairness, individuals in professional services go to college for a technical reason: to become engineers, environmental scientists, architects, planners, accountants, or lawyers—not to become salespeople and not necessarily to learn new ways of thinking and approaching things. It takes vision and experience in implementing growth strategies to light the kind of fire under them that propels them into growth mode.

THE LONELY MARKETER

I know a prominent marketing director from a sixty-person engineering firm on Long Island, New York. Because neither principals nor staff members are engaged in any kind of growth process, the marketing director does everything. She develops client relationships through multiple face-to-face meetings and undertakes follow-up meetings to sign clients. She works with them to develop opportunities, determine the scope of work to be done, and present contracts. When she brings questions back to the office, the firm's principals help her address technical issues that are not her bailiwick (although frankly, I'm not sure what *isn't* her bailiwick!), but they do not get involved in selling, preferring to remain strictly technical people.

Given the depth and scope of her responsibilities, I asked her how big the firm was now as opposed to ten years ago. She responded that it was about the same.

I then inquired about the firm's turnover rate, assuming that with the kind of outreach she was doing, it would be low.

"We have a very high turnover rate," she answered. "We're always having people leave. We're always hiring new people."

So the firm was not growing, and its principals didn't want to take responsibility for generating new business, instead putting the onus on a lone marketing person with limited technical education and understanding. Apparently, she is one of very few in the firm with any level of motivation, burdened with keeping the firm afloat—but apparently not ascendant, try as she might.

PRESSURE AND PREROGATIVES

Another consequence of no growth is poor client retention and vulnerability to client whims. Clients may change their procurement practices, or they may suddenly require new skill sets for their technical needs. If a company sustains itself strictly on a loyal client base, and for some reason a client moves to a competitor, that client can be very hard to replace.

The risk that a client may leave rises if the client has become attached to a single employee—for example, a principal or senior project manager. The client may have more allegiance to the individual than to the firm as a whole, possibly because the firm has not taken the time to introduce the client to other employees with different skill sets. The client then associates the firm with expertise on whatever specific service is being provided by that principal or senior project manager, and looks elsewhere when thinking about a different project with different requirements.

If the principal with the client relationship leaves to start up a new firm, or the senior project manager leaves for any other reason, the client may easily follow that individual out. So not only does the firm in a no-growth mode lose a staff member, it also loses a client. Vulnerability to client whims is also a problem when catering to price-sensitive clients, whose focus is on always trying to do things for less. This squeezes margins, increases overhead, and diminishes the staff's opportunities to work on diverse and stimulating projects.

ADAPTING AND SHIFTING: COMMODITIZATION

A significant consequence of lack of growth is an inability to adapt to evolving client needs. Talent and skills tend to be static in a firm that doesn't grow, and when new technologies come along, the employees of such firms often do not become familiar with them quickly enough. Clients expect you to keep current and may turn to your competitors if they sense that you are not. A firm caught in this predicament will sometimes offer to get up to speed, but it may not be able to change quickly enough to provide what's needed. And it becomes harder to adapt when you have lots of people stuck in their roles without opportunities for advancement.

Not anticipating and preparing for market shifts is another, extremely dangerous consequence of failure to grow. Uber and Lyft are stellar examples of companies that seized the day when it came to market shifts, and I will talk about them later in the chapter. In his book *The Fourth Industrial Revolution*, World Economic Forum founder Klaus Schwab makes the case that in the digital age, the period of change we are living through is more significant, and the ramifications of the latest technological revolution more immense, than any prior period of human history.

"The changes are so profound," he says, "that from the perspective of human history, there has never been a time of greater promise or potential peril. My concern, however, is that decision-makers are too often caught in traditional, linear (and non-disruptive) thinking or too absorbed by immediate concerns to think strategically about the forces of disruption and innovation shaping our future."[2]

In the digital age, we're witnessing a dramatic evolution of artificial intelligence (AI)—robots that are able to do the jobs humans do, such as taking items off the shelf, packing them in boxes, and shipping them from a warehouse. By the time the item ends up at your doorstep, the driver who delivers might be virtually the only human being who has been involved. But with the use of drones as delivery vehicles, even that is changing.

Because change is happening so fast, there is concern that common classes of jobs—retail salespeople in stores; medical personnel; people who do the field data collection common in engineering and archi-

---

2 Klaus Schwab, *The Fourth Industrial Revolution* (New York: Crown Business, 2017), 2–3.

tecture—will soon go away. Drones are used increasingly for aerial surveillance of freeways, which means that traffic reporters and the helicopter pilots who escort them will one day fade away too. But the professional services industry is historically very slow to recognize these changes and adapt to them.

Very large firms with five thousand to ten thousand employees have whole departments that track trends and figure out ways to adapt. But 90 percent of the firms in this country lack the resources and ability to adapt in this way, which makes them susceptible to the kinds of market shifts outlined in Schwab's book—and if they are unprepared, they could conceivably go out of business. With the mentality that being in a Good Enough Zone is, well, *good enough*, failure becomes destiny rather than something they can anticipate and avoid.

To date, Uber and Lyft are the companies that have best exploited market shifts in the transit industry. They have left traditional taxis in the dust, all because they saw around corners when smartphone development disrupted the way people do things. Uber and Lyft understood that hundreds of thousands of apps are available to anyone with a smartphone, and that such apps are easy for technology companies to create—meaning that getting from point A to point B was a new multibillion-dollar industry waiting to happen. Sure, these companies have had growing pains, but the bottom line is that they saw what was coming and were able to capitalize on it. Unfortunately, taxi companies did not see this coming. Had they operated in a less shortsighted manner, they might have identified this trend and adapted to it.

This example demonstrates how professional services firms can and will become victims of external disruption unless they decide to pay attention and evolve. That in itself is an opportunity and a challenge: how do you do this if you're a small firm? There are ways to anticipate market shift, putting safe growth strategies into place, which we will explore further on in the book. These can include studying other companies that are thought leaders, seeing what has worked for them, noting the mistakes they have made, and striving to avoid those mistakes.

Understanding why changes are occurring, deciding which innovations look as though they're sustainable, and determining how they apply to your firm are all important components of growth. And this can be done without a huge, risky investment.

At the annual American Council of Engineering Companies (ACEC) Conference, I taught a seminar on how firms of all sizes can anticipate and adapt to market shifts—how to size up what's going on not only within your industry, but also outside of it. That information is part of any *safe growth* strategy.

SOCIAL CHANGE: A CONSCIENCE BY ANY OTHER NAME

Growth and adaptation to change require more than just a willingness to keep abreast of trends in technology and consumer behavior. Society is changing, and in the last couple of decades, more and more individuals—including prospective talent and clients—have opted to work for and with firms that have a social conscience over those that don't. In their 2007 book *Firms of Endearment: How World Class Companies Profit from Passion and Purpose*, authors Rajendra Sisodia, David B. Wolfe, and Jagdish N. Sheth introduced the concept of *conscious leadership* and suggested that "humane" companies are the ones blazing the fastest trails to the top. Long-term competitive advantage, the authors posit, is measured in terms of value that matters: emotional, experiential, social, and financial.[3]

Another of Sisodia's books, *Conscious Capitalism: Liberating the Heroic Spirit of Business*, coauthored with Whole Foods CEO John Mackey, takes the theme of socially responsible business practices even further. Sisodia and Mackey both sit on the board of directors of Conscious Capitalism, an organization dedicated to promoting ethical, sustainable business practices, and the notion that such practices are good for business—and these values are catching on: today Conscious Capitalism has forty chapters worldwide.

When you think about change and innovation, which lead to growth, it's impossible to overlook the impact a social conscience has on a business, especially when thriving businesses in the S&P 500 are embracing these values.

A commitment to growth can lead to a sustainable business that attracts and retains human capital and fuels demand for company stock ownership. Ideally, firms should look at growing from every angle, but even executing one or two strategies can enable you to stay relevant. Of course you also need to be able to effectively execute those strategies without getting caught up in the day-to-day demands of your business, something I'll discuss in the next chapter.

---

3   Rajendra Sisodia, David B. Wolfe, and Jagdish N. Sheth, *Firms of Endearment* (Philadelphia: Wharton School Publishing, 2007).

CHAPTER 3

DON'T LOSE FOCUS

You have worked hard for many years to build your company, and you know that a lot of things can sabotage your success. You understand that nothing is more important to you than managing your business. So why does it sometimes seem so hard to maintain focus on this task?

Don't worry, you aren't alone in this. My survey of more than three thousand executives in the A/E and environmental industry identified three primary reasons that executives' attention is diverted to other things.

The leading reason is that they get lost in the day-to-day requirements of their jobs and don't have time to think long-term. Most executives, after a long, distinguished career working their way up the ladder, tend to keep their hands in the business's creative work. But in a management role, it can be very difficult to balance doing the work and running the business.

Losing sight of the big picture because you're caught up in ground-level, daily tasks imperils strategic vision and execution. It makes an executive "strategically myopic." This is dangerous, because when crises happen, they often occur suddenly and without warning, and when they do, you don't want to be caught flat-footed.

Fred Kramer, AIA, ran a profitable architecture firm before selling it to Stantec, where he now serves as vice president and east regional business leader/buildings. He offers this perspective:

> "One of the mistakes was not doing strategic planning when markets were good and we were busy. In other words, 'We don't need to strategic plan right now, everything's fine, Fred.' I would say, 'No, if you're doing your strategic plan in a crisis, your ability to invest is going to be compromised. When the crisis requires bringing in work tomorrow, we are going to be in trouble.'"

> "So in the midst of a crisis is not the time to do a strategic plan. You have to have tactics tomorrow if you are desperate. Strategic planning should not be done from a position of desperation. Usually, the best time to do a strategic plan is when everybody's hair is on fire [from too much work]."

The second reason that executives lose their focus on the business is that staff themselves don't have business management experience. Like you, your staff members have likely become company leaders because they have excelled at their work. However, technical accomplishment doesn't necessarily translate to management or leadership excellence. Even the most proficient executives still need their subordinates to have some level of business acumen. Otherwise, growth plans get sidetracked.

And number three is organizational confusion, whereby staff are uncertain about what the organization's business strategies are and where they fit in. As a result, instead of devoting extra attention to management, they just stick to their day-to-day jobs, helping to win new work when they are called upon and delivering that work to clients. This is good, but it should be achieved *alongside* strategy execution, not in lieu of it.

The problem of organizational confusion is magnified when a long string of acquisitions creates an enormous, bloated company with a lot of talented people but a mismatch of corporate and departmental objectives and direction. As Fred Kramer attests:

> "The buildings group at Stantec that I am part of was two thousand people when we joined Stantec three years ago. It's four thousand people today. Stantec didn't have a consolidated strategic plan for buildings. And I'm going, "What?" That's not really sustainable, because you don't keep your best people. They leave because they don't know where the company is going. Because of all this, we have a lot to learn. So we're [the buildings group] literally going through our first strategic plan now.

> "It's hard. If every single sector had its own vision and its own strategy, then that means there's no vision and strategy for the whole. I think there needs to be one for the whole and the others need to feed into it in some way. They can't be contrary to one another. That's where we're having a bit of a challenge, but the effort is well worth it."

If you can overcome all three of these challenges, you will be in a position to develop key management strategies and create new opportunities for your business. Ultimately, you'll be able to create the necessary momentum to ensure that there is always a line of new customers and prospects in whatever area your strategy targets.

It won't be easy, but it can be manageable. Let's look more closely at each of these three problems and how to handle them.

PROBLEM #1: THE WEEDS

Success begins (and ends) in the weeds. Daily details are important, but you still need to maintain a 360-degree view of everything. You must allocate time to learn what is going on—to know where the potential trouble spots are and where opportunity lies. It's important to remember that when small issues go unnoticed and unresolved while you're stuck in the routine demands of the job, they can quickly blow up into large problems. Problems that are left unchecked soon snowball until they crush your business.

Lisa Brothers, PE, LEED AP, ENV SP, CEO and chairman of Nitsch Engineering, says:

> "One of the things about strategy, which I tell people all the time: people always pay attention to the urgent, but not the important. The urgent is in front of you every single day. If you never pick your head up from the urgent and make time for the strategy, it's never going to happen. So, by having the plan and having the action plan with quarterly check-ins, having multiple people responsible for it, never postponing it, and always making it important, it makes everybody lift their head up. They then think about the strategy. Then people know where we're headed and can help us build it."

There are several reasons to be vigilant about what's going on in the company. First and foremost, your competitors are waiting for you, your firm, and your staff to screw up. They are prepared to seize your moment of weakness, and if you aren't careful, you and your company can end up on the outside looking in.

Another threat is posed by recruiters who are trying to steal employees. Even in slow times, the AEC and environmental industry have historically experienced robust hiring. I know of no AEC or environmental professional, even at the height of a recession, who had to wait long to find a new job after being laid off. When it comes to engineering and environmental consulting, there is always a war for talent, and those who overlook that fact end up on the losing end. When the economy is thriving, you can be assured that your competition is using recruiters to try to lure your most treasured staff away from you. Are your employees happy? If not, then you are vulnerable.

If you're mired in the day-to-day minutiae of your job, what's happening to your clients? Do you know if they are getting the attention and service they deserve? What do your clients think of your company? Do they still like your firm better than your competitors, who are surely working diligently to lure your clients away? If there are slip-ups, miscommunications, quality issues, or staffing problems, clients can very quickly turn to another firm. All of these things can happen when you're stuck in the weeds and not paying attention to trouble spots that may be brewing. Make sure you allocate some time to the big picture every single day.

PROBLEM #2: STAFF IS NOT SKILLED IN BUSINESS SCIENCE

Outside of the CEO's office, most organizations don't have enough people who understand business growth and organizational behavior. This shouldn't come as a surprise. After all, most employees in engineering/architectural/environmental services are there because of their technical expertise and experience. Most are focused on the technical challenges presented by their jobs, not business issues.

However, it's important that everyone in the organization contributes to managing the business. Just as everyone in the organization contributes to the success of the firm's projects, they must also be focused on the firm's long-term success.

Without business skills, though, their efforts are often misdirected. Employees who aren't adequately trained in this area often impede progress rather than move the business forward.

The problem begins early, in college. Engineering, architectural, and most science curricula have virtually no business learning requirements—no finance, marketing, legal, organizational behavior, or human resources classes. At most, students may be exposed to a handful of electives. The typical graduate leaves school with no business foundation, and the best he or she can hope for is to learn how to run the business on the job.

The result is an industry full of professionals who tend to treat their business-related responsibilities like one of their projects. There's a preliminary design phase, where they investigate what to do. They then design it, pick a solution, and pursue it. After that, they cross their fingers and hope that everything is going to work out just fine. Unlike a typical project, they have ventured far outside their core expertise.

Those with business training know that running the business first starts with people. Employees must feel that they are given clear direction, that they know what to do, and that they're certain of the outcome. They also want to feel confident that they will be able to overcome any resistance or fears from within the organization. These are not technical topics; these are people topics. But it's an area where staff—even senior management—typically have no training, aside from a few in departments like accounting, marketing, and human resources.

Moreover, those professionals who *do* have a background in business are not leveraged effectively. Rarely do you see marketing, accounting, or HR sitting at the boardroom table. You might sometimes see them on the management team, but usually just in a support role. Few firms give these business-educated players leadership roles that enable them to guide and advise staff on strategic business matters.

For instance, all too often human resources is relegated to administering employee benefits and participating in onboarding and exiting staff. Accounting is usually focused on looking in the rearview mirror to study what's already happened—billings, revenue, cash, expenses, and bookings. Rarely is accounting allowed to forecast and advise about what's to come and counsel company leaders how to overcome barriers to growth. This starts to be an exception only as a firm approaches five hundred or so employees—according to the US Census Bureau, that group comprises less than 10 percent of all professional services firms.

Likewise, marketing departments are also typically confined to a support role. Junior people with limited experience are managing web pages, databases, proposal production, résumés, conferences, and product and services brochures. These are not business leadership activities. They are not developing performance metrics or coaching technical staff to employ contemporary business processes to generate more revenue.

Even those who serve in operations roles are frequently technical professionals who have been promoted. Their role is often to decide when to hire and when to fire, and to look at the day-to-day details of who's working on what project. Operations managers rarely model future needs or predict changing needs to ensure continuity in the positions, ensure uniform progression of employees' skills to support their success in more complex senior roles, or understand the organizational behavior elements of employee morale and motivation.

One of the most commonly missed opportunities for effective management that I have observed is in manpower projections. When a surge of business hits the books, staffing managers find themselves scrambling to bring new people on board. The trouble is, that is too late. The process of identifying new hire candidates can take many months and even more than a year. Meanwhile, the staffing shortage in the firm results in overworked, burned-out staff and missed contractual deadlines. During such times, sales, marketing, and strategy execution move to the back burner. This negatively impacts the firm's profitability as bookings shrink and turnover increases.

This situation can be avoided if the managers understand how to forecast staffing needs. Many firms attempt to forecast needs by tracking booked backlog: the business under contract but not yet completed. However, backlog is constantly burned and is not a good predictor of future business.

Some firms take advantage of opportunity tracking systems by applying a success factor to the value of opportunities in the system, and adding this to the firm's backlog total to arrive at a revenue projection. I call this an intermediate revenue indicator, which is better, but still inadequate.

What technical staff members don't realize is that by measuring opportunities, lead generation, and new client relationship development activities, they can forecast staffing needs far in advance of opportunity- or backlog-based projections. These early sales indicators often double the timeframe for projecting staffing needs.

I developed such a system using client relationship management (CRM) software and time sheet coding to track early sales activities and to trend the data. I call it the Revenue Forecasting Tool (RFT). With the RFT, I have been able to forecast more than a year beyond what backlog projections could accomplish. However, if your technical staff aren't business-savvy, such techniques will be lost on them. They're not business professionals and therefore can rarely serve as financial modelers or understand or have confidence in early sales activities.

PROBLEM #3: CONFUSING STRATEGIES, UNCLEAR DIRECTION

When the CEO and management team have their heads down working on projects, day-to-day emergencies, and staffing issues, they aren't looking at the big picture and they probably aren't communicating the business strategic vision to staff. Or worse, maybe the strategy hasn't even been effectively determined. Maybe a handful of competing strategic objectives are creating an inefficient jumble and causing different executives, departments, and personnel to step on each other's toes.

If a coherent, overarching strategy—one that works for the organization as a whole, as well as its constituent parts—is not clearly and persistently communicated by the CEO and upper management, it deters employees from participating in business process improvements and adaptation. Without the necessary buy-in from staff, those efforts fall by the wayside.

Moreover, a lack of communication about priorities can sow confusion and induce strategic paralysis. If the leadership and the employees are communicatively out of sync, employees feel less motivated to innovate and to try out new methods. Therefore, even when new methods or approaches are rolled out, they often go nowhere because staff see the initiatives as a waste of their time that will take them away from their day-to-day job.

LET TECHNOLOGY SERVE YOU—
NOT THE OTHER WAY AROUND

While technology is essential for the smooth operation of a business, sometimes firm leaders grow too reliant on it. They abdicate some of their leadership responsibilities to the technology. For instance, accounting software is terrific at spitting out utilization reports. Utilization is an important key performance indicator (KPI) reflecting the firm's billable/nonbillable ratio established in the annual business plan's budget. However, when staff are inundated with these reports—monthly, weekly, and sometimes even daily—it becomes easy for them to focus excessively on utilization at the expense of sales, on which most strategies depend.

The unintended consequence is that those KPIs that are most often discussed become the focus, at the expense of revenue generation and other critical business activities. A simple but effective fix I made for one firm that was concentrated too heavily on utilization was to change the operations meeting agenda so that utilization was near the last page, instead of the first page. Since meetings tend to run long, this approach squeezed the utilization discussion while shifting the focus to revenue generation, conflict resolution, and people management, which were discussed earlier in the meeting.

THE BEST DEFENSE IS A GOOD OFFENSE

Guard your firm against potential threats by maintaining a concerted focus on management. Make time to look at the big picture. Talk to people within and outside the firm, look at all external influences, and learn how to spot trouble before it becomes a problem.

If you accomplish these things, your staff will follow suit. You'll now have multiple ears and eyes to augment the company's ability to notice threats and opportunities and respond to them. Your employees will also recognize that the business processes you are introducing are supported throughout the organization and they will more readily support those processes and adapt to the change identified in your strategic plan.

Needless to say, achieving these things necessitates effective leadership. "Leadership" is a word that's bandied about all the time in the upper echelons of the corporate world, but what does it really mean? More importantly, how does one lead effectively? Chapter 4 will provide the answers.

CHAPTER 4

START A MOVEMENT

In previous chapters, we identified the purpose of growth. It is not growth for growth's sake, nor is it necessarily measured in terms of more employees, more revenue, and more profit. It is about continuous, organization-wide dedication to improvement. We must do anything to avoid the Good Enough Zone.

The ability of a firm to advance strategy falls squarely on its leader's shoulders. "The implementation of a strategic plan is the CEO's responsibility to make sure it's happening and moving forward," says Lisa Brothers of Nitsch Engineering. "It's nobody else's responsibility but the CEO's. It's the primary role. If you don't know how to lead, learn. It's an indispensable skill that will pay dividends over the entire course of your career."

Strategy execution requires leaders who can arouse excitement for the cause and inspire followers to join up with passion and energy. Many A/E firm leaders lack confidence in their ability to lead. If you practice the methods described in this chapter and those that follow, you will surprise yourself with what you are capable of achieving.

Before delving into our study of leadership, it's important to recognize the difference between leadership and management. Leadership is the art of motivating a group of people to act toward achieving a common goal. Management is the act or skill of controlling and making decisions about an entity. Growing a business requires being both a leader and a manager. Al Curran, PE, co-founder of Top ENR 100 engineering and operations firm Woodard & Curran, says:

> "Being able to support people to pursue the thing they are best at is more of a leadership attribute than a management attribute. So many people who end up in leadership roles, especially in our business, get there based on being good managers, but without understanding how to transition from being a manager to a leader. They really need to study leadership to discover their own personal leadership strength."

It really is not that complicated. There are just four components: leaders succeed if they keep strategies simple, if their actions are visible, if they embrace their team members as equals, and if their vision is widely seen as worthy. Following this playbook will allow them to execute strategy proficiently—and maybe even start a movement.

FROM LONE NUT TO LEADER: FOUR STEPS TO "STARTING A MOVEMENT"

In his enthralling talk at TED2010, Derek Sivers offered a perfect, succinct example of what it means to build a movement. In the presentation, Sivers narrates commentary over a crude cell phone video taken at an outdoor concert. In the span of two minutes, a fearless leader steps up, initiates an action, and persuades dozens to follow suit.

In this video, a young man, the Leader, rises and begins dancing in a wild and crazy manner, utterly alone, with no one around him. Is he a nut? He is certainly acting silly. But he's clearly in his element and enjoying himself to the fullest.

A minute into it, a second person (the First Follower) rises and joins him. The Leader and the First Follower dance around each other, in the same unabashedly silly fashion as before. Now, with the involvement of the First Follower (who is, in a sense, a leader himself), the little gathering is starting to show some promise. But will it grow? Or is it just two nuts?

Less than a minute later, a third man joins the other two in their dance. As Sivers points out, this is a critical turning point: "three's a crowd." Seconds later, multiple people join the party, and now that the group has gained momentum, the floodgates are thrown open: even *more* people flock to the gathering, all of them dancing enthusiastically to the music.

In his analysis of this video, Sivers makes several excellent points about leadership that we can apply to the field of strategy execution. If no one had joined the first guy, he wouldn't have been a leader; he'd simply have been a lone nut. The First Follower made the lone dancer's activities appear legitimate. The Leader and the First Follower both took great risk of being ridiculed. But by the time a handful of people had gathered, there was no longer any risk for newcomers to join. In fact, once the group reached a certain size, the pressure was on for those who chose to remain sitting. They had become the outsiders and were now at risk of being "uncool."

The context of the story couldn't be farther from the buttoned-up world of the corporate boardroom, but the lessons are easily applicable for any leaders who wish to improve their firm by heading up an organizational strategy. In any setting, a leader is not a leader until he or she has followers; the leader must treat followers as equals; and the activity to which the leader recruits followers must be simple, highly visible, and seen as worthy.

Let's explore real-life examples of these principles at work—and how leaders fail when they don't uphold them.

THE PERIL OF FLIP-FLOPPING:

As governor of New Jersey, Chris Christie was hailed as an effective leader. He grew the economy and, for a while, deftly managed the state government. Riding on the wave of this success, his focus transitioned to national politics when he competed for the presidential nomination in the 2016 Republican primaries. During this campaign, he took strong positions against fellow candidate Donald Trump and was a vocal critic of Trump in the papers and on television.

Once Trump won the nomination, Christie equivocated on earlier statements. Instead of leveling pointed criticism at Trump, he came out eagerly to defend the presidential candidate. The governor's goal, it was widely thought, was to curry favor with Trump so he would be picked as Trump's running mate or nominated to a high-level federal position should Trump eventually win the election.

This backfired. Christie was ridiculed for being weak and opportunistic, and he was even called a puppet of the candidate. Because of this and other scandals that rocked New Jersey state government, his reputation took a dramatic hit. The one-time rising star of the GOP had been disgraced and discredited as a leader, and his governorship ended with his approval rating in the cellar.

Christie made many mistakes. His flip-flops signaled that he was not confident in his strategy, and that he was a shameless opportunist. Although Christie was highly visible, this visibility worked against him. In fact, his most visible action as governor ended up being his role in the "Bridgegate" scandal that contributed to his downfall. By this point, most of his initial followers had abandoned him.

In a short time, Christie had gone from rising star with White House ambitions to a beleaguered "lone nut."

YOU CAN'T WIN FOLLOWERS WITHOUT A WORTHY CAUSE

The new CEO of an A/E firm enthusiastically led his team through a strategic planning process. One of the goals was to boost recruiting. A tactic to achieve this strategic goal was to make the company be seen as a desirable place to work.

Shortly after the planning process, a local business newspaper launched its annual Best Employer contest. The CEO seized on this as an opportunity to achieve the recognition that would spark an influx of higher-quality job applicants to support the planned growth.

To qualify for the award, not only did the employees have to attest to the company being a great employer, the rules required that 50 percent of the employees participate.

The CEO sent out an email to the employees excitedly telling them about the contest and how they could log in and answer the survey questions that were part of the contest. Then, he traveled to each of the company's four offices and met with the employees to ask them to participate.

As the deadline drew near, the CEO logged in to check on progress. The company had achieved nowhere near the 50 percent benchmark. He then vigorously doubled down on his efforts, beseeching the employees to participate. But to no avail.

Frantic, he begged, "Please take the survey! We need to win!"

Alas, the employees did not listen, and the firm didn't meet the eligibility requirements for the contest.

The problem here was twofold. One was that the employees saw no personal benefit to take the time to fill out the survey. The benefit was only for the owners of the company. Second and more importantly, the firm was simply not a good employer. It was a white collar company that treated its employees like they were blue collar (and openly said so). Its retention was commensurately terrible.

The lesson is that the cause—winning the contest—was not seen as worthy. In fact, employees didn't even believe the company *deserved* to win. They knew their employer was far from "the best company to work for," and the employees were not going to participate because they did not want to.

Mistakes like those of Chris Christie and this A/E firm CEO have doomed countless political and business leaders. Now let's look at a case of leadership success.

SEEING IS BELIEVING

An East Coast engineering and planning firm, Hoyle, Tanner & Associates, began to focus on invigorating its future under a new CEO, Chris Mulleavey, PE, who had risen to the top after being with the firm for almost twenty years. This new CEO was progressive and believed in motivating staff by allowing them to make decisions and control their own destiny.

The CEO retained my firm, FosterGrowth, to lead the multiyear strategic planning and execution process. First, we involved employees who were seen as socially influential: not just those with a title, but the ones whose opinions were respected by their peers. The fact that they had followers demonstrated their leadership qualities.

Next, I conducted a workshop with the strategic planning team to make sure that all participants understood the ins and outs of achieving growth. Then we identified each participant's personal motivation for working with the firm. From this collection of personal motivations, we built a new company vision statement that emphasized empowering employees by aligning their individual motivations with the objectives of the company.

This approach was the complete opposite of the values of one of my A/E employers, which didn't seem to care about what was in it for the employees and was only interested in using its employees as a means to an end. Instead, what we were doing at this firm was true empowerment, built on strategies that each participant saw as worthy.

The next step was to make this fact highly visible to catalyze the involvement of all the other employees. The "energy" of empowerment is infectious and encourages active, enthusiastic participation from all members of an organization—just like the dancer at the concert had a "contagious" effect on those who noticed he was having a great time.

Companies often create a visible theme around elements of the strategic plan. For example, Lamp, Rynearson displayed a colorful, large-scale infographic that described the organization's goals and journey. At Hoyle, Tanner, a dazzling four-quadrant graphic was created using images connected to each strategic goal. Even better, the image had an embedded link for each goal that displayed the company's progress against that goal. The following is a grey-scale of the graphic:

Mouse Pad with the dual purpose of a digitally linked progress report

First, the graphic was printed on a circular mouse pad for distribution to all employees. It doesn't get much more "visible" than that, considering how much time you spend in front of your computer each day. But the company took it a step further: it wasn't just some intern who distributed the mouse pads, but the CEO of the company, who traveled to each of the firm's six offices and personally handed them out, along with each employee's bonus check.

This was no mere gimmick—it served to communicate in a powerful, memorable, public way that upper management expected every employee to contribute to and benefit from the success of the strategic plan. It showed that the plan was worthy, both individually and on the corporate level.

Such demonstrations can be inspiring and motivating, but one-time events risk losing their shine once the spectacle is over. To maintain focus and to fuel continued support among employees, the mouse pad was turned into a living progress report. The strategic plan implementation committee, which I was coaching, created a spreadsheet style-progress report. Then, an imaginative employee created a "live" PDF that described each of the goals on a digital image of the mouse pad and was embedded with a hyperlink to the progress report.

The mouse pad graphic thus became an updatable progress report that was made available to all employees on the company's intranet. Further, the firm held periodic "town meetings" where all employees were invited to hear about progress on the plan from the execution team. The graphic was used in the presentation and viewed across the firm's video conferencing system.

"Seeing is believing," the saying goes, and this is especially true if you're a leader who wants to recruit followers. If your actions are visible and seen as worthy, others will believe in your mission.

RULES FOR LEADERS

When it comes to leadership and strategy execution, you don't need to reinvent the wheel. Learn from the failures and triumphs of leaders who have preceded you, and follow these time-tested rules.

1. First, we must examine our motivation. Ask, "Does the outcome serve us only or are the benefits shared widely?" Selfish goals are likely connected to ego. Ego is all about oneself. And staff sees right through this.

A less egotistical approach is to show some vulnerability and empathy. Try it and see how people respond. Do less telling and more listening and asking questions of others. This way, you will gain a lot more respect as a leader.

Ego pushes people away. It causes others to lose faith in the mission. Would-be followers start thinking in "every man for himself" terms instead of about the good of the organization. After all, they reason, if the executives are working only for their own benefit, why should we struggle and strive?

The rewards of taking part in a project or program should be widely shared. As Adam Grant, author and Wharton professor, writes, "The most meaningful way to succeed is to help others succeed."[4] In the context of strategy execution, if others perceive your objective to be meaningful and worthy, you're on the right track.

2. Can the goal be expressed simply? This means defining the goal in terms that convey its worthiness, which likely goes deeper than just "make more money" and instead offers career satisfaction and engagement in enjoyable, challenging projects. Think of the example of the dancing man. People saw his objective—launch a spontaneous dance party!—as exciting. Surely, he was visibly enjoying his solitary dance in the beginning, even before the First

---

4 Adam Grant, *Give and Take: Why Helping Others Drives Our Success* (New York: Penguin Books, 2014).

Follower came along. But he also clearly wanted others to enjoy the same.

3. Who might be your first and second followers? Talk to them. Test your ideas on them. Seek out at least one person who has a track record of being highly critical. That person may at first tear your idea apart, but this is a good test and helps you pinpoint weaknesses before a broader group has a chance to see them. Once a highly critical person is on board, they often become your most steadfast champion.

   Anticipate that many direct reports react to suggestions for improvement as a criticism of their performance. It is important to convey your confidence in their ability and to express that hammering out strategic ideas is part of the learning process. Make sure they understand that by involving them, you are demonstrating that you value them and would like them to be part of that learning process to achieve a strong business outcome.

   If you display openness, allow dialogue, respect differing opinions, reward group problem solving, and foster a positive environment, you'll earn the loyalty of staff. Their trust in you is essential for executing any kind of strategy.

4. Be prepared to take full responsibility for the outcome. From the beginning, know that blaming is not an effective leadership trait. Look what happened in the Bridgegate scandal when Chris Christie blamed the obstruction of the George Washington Bridge on others—his self-serving attempt to deflect responsibility only deepened the hole he

was in and further eroded his leadership status in the eyes of his supporters.

5.   Stick to it. Plan the plan. Prepare to support its implementation. Understand and express your commitment often. Convey your dedication to providing support throughout implementation.

If a leader acts cheap, staff will emulate cheap; if he or she acts all-knowing, staff will feel that they have to act all-knowing and to solve all business problems themselves. Instead, acknowledge that no one knows everything and encourage the search for knowledge and skills externally (such as by consulting outside business professionals).

I'm grateful for having been exposed to external business experts on many topics over the course of my career: business organization experts, strategy experts, former CEOs of larger firms, corporate governance experts, financial strategists, and others. This has boosted my knowledge and honed my expertise.

External resources will teach staff what they don't know, keep them on track, and keep them out of trouble. Show the staff that knowledge is power.

Now you understand the right mindset for putting a plan in action. It starts with leadership. It starts with you. Tell yourself, "I am not just going to execute a strategy. I am going to start a movement."

Of course, even with a capable leader, a movement can't get very far without the right people supporting it. The following chapter teaches you how to identify and mobilize your allies—and how to handle people within the organization who might resist your plans.

CHAPTER 5

WHO CONTRIBUTES?

The CEO and the management team can't implement strategy in a vacuum. They need broader support. They need to be able to identify who in the company will buy in first and most eagerly, who will energize others to follow suit, and who might drag their feet and put up resistance.

ANTICIPATE YOUR INFLUENCE GROUPS

In their classic MBA program textbook *Essentials of Organizational Behavior*, Stephen Robbins and Timothy Judge describe three categories of people who impact the advancement of an initiative. [5] I call the three categories Early Adopters, "Wait and Seers," and Resisters.

---

5   Stephen P. Robbins and Timothy A. Judge, *Essentials of Organizational Behavior* (New York: Pearson, 2016).

In any major initiative, all three categories are represented among staff. It is best to recognize this up front and prepare for it.

Those who are quick to jump on board are the Early Adopters. Early Adopters have an open mind and they find new activities exciting rather than intimidating. These people buy into the cause and have sufficient confidence in themselves to implement the initiative. Moreover, their enthusiasm is infectious: they encourage others to do the same, especially if the Early Adopters are respected and liked by their peers.

Create a list of the Early Adopters and regard them as your teammates who will support your cause. Focus on them early on to cement their support. These individuals could end up being future leaders in the company and it's good to identify them early in the process.

The other two categories (Wait and Seers and Resisters) comprise "the opposition." Overcoming opposition to change is fundamental to executing strategy. It is important to understand who these individuals are and why they behave the way they do.

The "Wait and Seers" are not convinced the cause is worth it. They think the risks of personal involvement outweigh the benefits. Outwardly, they might give mixed messages about their true feelings and maybe even offer tepid expressions of support. But inwardly, they're skeptical.

They will try to avoid voicing any kind of explicit commitment toward a project. Their covert approach is to "wait and see" if the initiative has real legs. They likely have been burned before by investing substantial effort into a new cause only to have the firm abandon it later.

Leaders can turn Wait and Seers into supporters by being consistently firm and vocal about the importance and sustainability of the initiative. Leaders must also demonstrate through actions that those who help advance the cause are congratulated for their efforts. And leaders need to stand ready to provide support. The point is to convince the Wait and Seers that involvement offers great rewards and few risks. The goal is for the Wait and Seers to eventually buy in with the same enthusiasm as the Early Adopters.

The other faction of the opposition are the Resisters. They may or may not publicly decry the initiative, but they *will* work behind the scenes to undermine it. They will ridicule the initiative to coworkers, endlessly call attention to barriers, and even go behind others' backs to bad-mouth supporters, particularly the Early Adopters and the change leaders.

This is the most difficult situation to resolve. One approach is for the CEO to ask trusted individuals to watch out for signs of "resistance." Then, the CEO must quickly confront Resisters and make it clear that such behavior is unacceptable and, if continued, might lead to consequences, including termination. The hard part is when the individual does not fall in line and the CEO has to deliver on that threat, and that may mean firing a very high-ranking person. Thus, accountability and quick action are the only solution.

THE SABOTEUR

I found myself in this situation at my former A/E employer, when the CEO was being manipulated by a Resister. I had led a complete transformation of the way my division (50 percent of the two hundred–person firm) sold A/E services. All of the firm's principals and senior staff had gone through an extensive sales training program that I arranged. I even hired a young marketing coordinator and trained her to be a sales coach to the twenty-three project managers and twelve principals in the division.

Within a few months I learned that the person who managed the second largest division of the company was complaining to other division managers and was lobbying the CEO to put my marketing coordinator back in the control of the marketing department. The Resister also refused to adopt any of the new sales processes we learned in the training.

My division enjoyed a large, loyal client whose business comprised 20 percent of the division's revenue. After positioning for a major project for over a year, we were scheduled to be interviewed by the client, the final step to be selected.

This Resister managed to worm her way into the first interview dry run. The dry run was rough, as it was the first. A few hours after the dry run, I was called to the CEO's office and learned that the division manager had gone to him and told him our very important pursuit was in disarray.

The CEO should have rebuked her and told her to stay out of it. But he didn't, and she began to directly interfere with our presentation planning. Ultimately, we still won the work, but the lead principal was so disillusioned that he resigned. I also left a few months later.

Two years later, with both me and the lead principal gone, the client fired the firm. Millions of dollars of annual revenue were lost. And it all started with one Resister— and a CEO who did not make her get on board with the new processes or address the obvious insecurity that motivated her obstructionist behavior.

A common cause of initiative failure is that CEOs often don't give power to punish (i.e. the ability to reprimand or fire) to the people whom they've entrusted to oversee an initiative. It is critical for the person leading the initiative to have the authority to apply consequences to bad actors who interfere with the firm's progress. Otherwise, everyone loses.

As you undertake a change strategy, anticipate these different reactions from different camps. Talk about it with the team. Ask them for sincere opinions. Speak with the Resisters and work to eliminate their fears. Let them know that it is not acceptable to just dig in their heels. If they feel that way, they should be removed from the team.

Finally, remember this: to get people to buy into a change process, two conditions must be satisfied: (1) individuals must believe that they are capable of making the change; and (2) the benefits to them outweigh the risk. To encourage enthusiastic support, you can utilize the six "influence elements" (discussed in Chapter 7), often with coaching, participation, and connecting to the individual's work motivation.

POSITIVE INFLUENCE

Not everyone in the firm has the same amount of influence on their peers. And just because someone has seniority or holds an important title doesn't mean that he or she has positive influence.

There are different kinds of influence. The weakest kind of influence is that which is bestowed by title. The most powerful influence is *social influence*.[6] Those with social influence can motivate people on a personal level. These people are highly socially engaged and have personal connections with a large number of employees at all levels in the firm. In essence, they're simply seen by coworkers as being cool. Find out who has that social influence in the firm and recruit them to help you support the new initiative.

The easiest way to find out who wields social influence is by conducting private meetings with individuals from a broad cross-section of the firm, including professionals of different ages and levels. Ask, "Who is the most respected? Whose opinion is listened to and whose isn't?"

Be careful not to talk to people who are considered "brown-nosers," as well as those whom staff don't trust or like. It can be useful to also find out who has low social standing, because having the wrong people identified as influencers could actually do damage. There may be people in the firm whose opinions are discounted by their peers.

Make sure you are discreet and respectful of all employees. Your purpose is not to denigrate anyone. Just focus on determining who has the most respect while avoiding those who are not respected.

As you search for the influencers, recognize that your direct reports may not be a reliable source of information. They may just be telling you what they think you want to hear, rather than what they really believe. Or, they may not really have their finger on the pulse of the company.

There are a number of less obvious ways to identify the young influencers in the firm. You just have to make the effort to speak with them on their terms.

---

6   Joseph Grenny, Kerry Patterson, David Maxfield, Ron McMillan, and Al Switzler. *Influencer: The New Science of Leading Change* (New York: McGraw-Hill Education, 2013).

LAUNCHING NEW LEADERS AT LUNCH

Not long ago, I was a division manager and shareholder of a regional A/E firm. I noticed that my peers got along fine and they often enjoyed social lunches with each other. But that did not extend to the millennials.

Occasionally, a millennial left the firm. Sometimes it was for maternity leave and other times it was for career opportunities. As is common in business, there was always a sendoff event, such as a lunch, dinner, or after-work drink. I made it a point to attend these and usually paid all or part of the tab, which I think is only fair, and I was happy to do it. Almost always, I was the only owner present.

During these events, staff often shared their opinions about what they liked and did not like about the firm. From these chats, I was able to discern who was constructive in their criticism and who was not, who had a good business mind and strong aspirations and who did not. I also saw how colleagues interacted with each other. It was clear to me who the influencers were.

During these gatherings, I sometimes struck deals with the group. They wanted to learn more about business or selling, so I offered to conduct a series of lunch lectures. The company often organized "brown bag" learning programs, but I learned that the part the millennials really objected to was the "brown bag" part. They resented that the company didn't even provide lunch when they were sacrificing their lunch hour to attend. I promised I would buy lunch if they promised to rally the "younger set" to attend.

They followed through on their end of the bargain and several of these young attendees quickly became major contributors to the company's sales effort. There was some backlash for me from the other owners about paying for lunch, but I knew that the ROI from the engagement of this group was huge, and I was happy to show a little appreciation for our dedicated millennial workers.

My engagement with them was tremendously beneficial because it helped me identify firsthand who the influencers were. Then, as I built relationships with them, they became my early adopters and contributors on long-term strategic initiatives.

Once you know who these employees are, it is important to sit down and have one-on-one conversations with them to validate their status as influencers and ask them to get involved in developing strategy for the firm. If you are able to add them to the roster of a strategic planning or other strategy development effort, you'll know you have the right people who will step up when it's time to implement your plan.

LOOK BEYOND THE USUAL SUSPECTS

When I'm retained to provide strategic planning services for a client, what I often receive from them, even before my agreement is signed, is a list of who the client wants to involve in the strategic planning effort. It's almost always a list of the most senior people in the firm—usually principals, division managers, and certain department managers.

Is this the best approach? Are these the most ambitious and committed individuals in the firm? Are there others who will one day be leaders or even owners? Aren't these people, regardless of where they might be on the hierarchy today, the future of your company?

I typically ask clients to hold off on communicating with or inviting anyone to the strategic planning team until completing what I, adapting some baseball terminology, call the "General Manager Prep." This is where I conduct face-to-face or online meetings with the CEO and C-suite members to identify what's motivating both the plan and the desired personal outcomes. They are aware of change, opportunities, and obstacles and have a sense if the timing is right to plan for the company's next three to five years.

At this stage, I introduce the idea that strategic planning must include key internal influencers—the ones who can jump-start the plan.

I once asked a CEO to consider who in his organization the opinion leaders were—people who were respected (whether they held positive or negative opinions) and who influenced others' thinking. I explained that they were the ones we needed to be on board with the plan. And I told him not to pay attention to seniority.

The CEO sent me a list of twenty-five participants for the strategic planning effort. The list included most principals, as well as the person who managed the print and document department, who issued plans and specifications for contractors and printed reports and specifications for the team. There were also two project engineers in the group.

The document manager was a person "in the know"; effectively the human water cooler. Everyone in the company who wanted to know anything about what was going on talked to her. She had her finger on the pulse of the organization and knew everything about everyone—both positive and negative. As soon as a management meeting concluded, she knew what was discussed, whether staff viewed it favorably or unfavorably, and if there was buy-in. People sought her out.

This was a wise choice and she turned out to be an active and stellar contributor during the entire strategic planning process.

Another choice was a project engineer who, two years into implementing the strategic plan, had risen from relative obscurity to a position of leadership in the firm. Throughout the planning process he was a solid contributor who advanced the cause and volunteered for lead roles on strategic plan action items.

One principal had been conspicuously omitted from the list. When I asked the CEO why, he responded that that individual wasn't well respected. He did a decent job, but wasn't likely to be listened to or lead any efforts.

Ultimately, the results showed that the CEO had succeeded in identifying the firm's most important influencers, as well as those who were unlikely to gel with the team. Since then, the company has grown substantially and has achieved record profits.

INFLUENCE IS NOT EQUAL TO SENIORITY

A one hundred-person engineering and planning firm conducted strategic planning following the guidance of influencers, or so we thought. It turns out that one of the members of the board of directors, who was also a practice leader and division manager, skipped out on the final strategic planning workshop to attend a meeting with a prospective client instead.

Six months after the completion of the strategic plan, the company was having trouble executing it. Not everybody was on board because many people didn't quite understand the goals. Despite the efforts of the CEO through memos, video conferencing sessions with all the offices, discussions at board meetings, and management meetings, the campaign seemed to lack buy-in. Several persons who had volunteered to lead some aspects of the mission voiced frustration to me.

I had breakfast with a board member to parse out what was interfering with the plan's execution. That was when I learned that the one board member had missed the final strategic planning workshop. When I went over a list of the goals, she said she did not understand what they meant. She didn't grasp why they were strategic, why they were important, or what the intended outcomes would be. I was astonished. Now I knew why the plan had stalled.

Fast-forward another year or two and we could see that this individual, while technically strong, was not influential in the business of the business. While the members of her team worked on projects with her, they didn't regard her as a mentor. Her lack of support and encouragement for team members led others on her team to emulate her and focus more on projects rather than strategy execution.

Any person on a board of directors is in a critical position to influence the direction of the firm, but their behavior dictates whether they are able to utilize that potential influence. Including this person in the strategic plan was a costly mistake, and a lot of time, money, and effort were wasted. Additionally, morale declined in the firm. It's fair to wonder why that person was even on the firm's board of directors, and it demonstrates why seniority, age, and prestige do not necessarily translate into the kind of social influence required for strategy execution.

YOUTH EQUALS ENERGY

When I was younger, I worked for an engineering and architectural firm with thirty-five employees in a single office. Our CEO was in his fifties and nearly everybody else was in their twenties and thirties. It was an unusually young group. I myself was a twenty-eight-year-old engineer.

We did not know that we were inexperienced and that we didn't have the credibility that comes with seniority. We charged full speed ahead, meeting directly with clients and prospects. I found that our clients loved us, partly because we were younger and partly because we were brash, worked hard, and had innovative ideas.

It seemed like we were constantly winning new business. We won so much work that in only two years the firm had grown to one hundred employees and diversified into mechanical and structural engineering.

Since then, I've always engaged the younger generation. Younger workers are often criticized for being lazy, unmotivated, clueless, or immature, but I've found this to be the exception rather than the rule. This is true also of the much-maligned millennials, whose work I have valued greatly. I have invited them to management meetings and have offered them important roles in projects, project pursuits, and strategic planning.

Youth equals energy. Young professionals have fewer preconceived notions and they don't have the perceived limitations that many long-time professionals have. All this talk about Millennials and Gen Xers being lazy is rubbish in my opinion. You just need to know what motivates them, such as empowerment. By the way, I know a lot of baby boomers who are lazy.

Young professionals are our future. When thinking about the influencers who would be involved with developing strategy, it's important to involve the influencers who are at an early point in their career and have the enthusiasm to help bring about change.

Utilization Barrier

There's one type of pushback that I often receive when I encourage using junior staff to help promote a strategic plan. Many firms think their younger professionals need to be solely focused on generating revenue. If firms have utilization goals of 95 to 100 percent for junior staff, how can they afford to involve them in overhead activities like strategic planning?

This is a very short-sighted attitude. When you speak with these junior influencers, you will find that their excitement level is high. They recognize that what you're asking them to do is important to their career, and that it's a real opportunity. As such, they will take this responsibility seriously—often more seriously than your senior staff will. If it's important to them, they're going to make it work. Ask them for commitment to maintain their utilization and they will likely oblige. Youth brings energy to the process. This generally means having a lot of capacity to contribute to the company, often even beyond the forty-hour work week.

So don't worry about utilization. Earn their loyalty and commitment by giving them a role in the strategic planning process. Engage them. It will pay off. It might even produce a few bright new leaders who will be the future of your firm.

Often, the best workers are those who are most well-rounded—the ones who excel not only in their area of technical expertise, but who have strategic chops and leadership skills too. In the next chapter, we'll look at how instilling business skills in technical staff can add enormous value to your workforce.

CHAPTER 6

BUSINESS SCIENCE: NOT JUST FOR BUSINESS PEOPLE

You're an architect in the performing arts business. You design theaters, amphitheaters, and stadiums. Business has been good, so you need to add some additional staff. As you're preparing your job ad, would you say, "Wanted: expert musician who wants to design theaters?" Probably not. You'd look for someone with training and experience designing theaters.

In most professional services firms, architects, scientists, planners, engineers, and other technical staff make up the majority of participants involved in strategic planning efforts, even though their expertise is in their respective technical fields. Professionals with business backgrounds—marketing, finance, and HR—are usually in the minority.

Building a strategy around people who aren't really trained to implement it might explain why so many strategic plans fail, since the final strategic plan represents the collective wisdom of people with limited business knowledge. However, the solution is not to exclude technical experts from strategy, but to give them the business knowledge that they lack. This approach makes your firm a force to be reckoned with because it expands the knowledge of your technical staff, giving them another weapon—business skills—to bolster their professional arsenal.

Let's examine a few real-life situations of strategic planning I have encountered. These are stories from CEOs who retained my services after their previous attempts at strategic planning had failed. One of the most important lessons they learned was the value of teaching business growth fundamentals to their entire strategic planning team *before* the strategic planning process even begins. This educational component is a centerpiece of my strategic planning program and one of the reasons why this program has produced so much success in a variety of firms.

IT'S NOT AS SIMPLE AS CUTTING A CHECK

Strategic Goal: Growth through acquisitions

Strategy Driver: Overcome mediocre stock performance

A regional architecture and engineering firm's senior management decided to hire a facilitator as part of the firm's strategic plan. The facilitator would interview employees, issue a memorandum on the desires and challenges identified during the interviews, and then conduct a full-day strategic planning workshop with twenty of the senior staff and principals. The facilitator had an MBA and years of experience providing strategic planning services and had even published a book on the topic.

Following the interviews, and after a day in a workshop with breakout groups and whiteboarding, the consultant helped the stakeholders achieve a consensus on the final strategic goals. One strategic goal was to grow the firm via acquisitions.

The plan was implemented, and after some time, the then-CEO had achieved the acquisition of five small firms of between ten and twenty-five employees. But trouble lurked around every corner.

The central problem was that the group believed acquisitions were an easy fix but did not have any real idea of what that entailed. They did not know the risks, nor did they understand the level of proficiency required in each of the corporate services groups—HR, marketing, IT, and finance—to integrate the acquisitions. In fairness, the facilitator had provided them with anecdotes about the risks versus rewards of acquisitions, but the message did not really sink in.

The strategic planning team did not understand what it meant to become fully integrated with the new employees and their clients—or how to partner with them to ease their transition. They did not even fully understand the acquired firms' existing problems at the time of purchase. The strategic planning team certainly learned about them later, when the team discovered, to their dismay, that most of the acquired firms had financial problems due to mismanagement or the recession. They didn't just acquire other companies—they acquired an entirely new set of challenges that they were ill-equipped to handle.

Ten years after the acquisitions campaign, the firm's financials had tanked. Four of the five acquired firms' offices were closed and only a handful of employees and original clients remained.

Really, You Really Need to Be Ready

There are several lessons in this story. An acquisition should never be pursued if growth is stalled due to weakness in internal processes and people at the parent firm. The facilitator had never implemented growth via an acquisition nor was it within his scope to teach business growth fundamentals to the team. Thus, the team made imprudent decisions using their limited business expertise. They went for what they perceived as an "easy fix" instead of rectifying their own shortcomings first.

Rather than going after expensive acquisitions, a senior business professional would have been able to spot the real problem. Then that person, or another person skilled at business training, could have engaged the group in a learning program. The team could have invested time to understand growth barriers and how to approach their own weak points, such as their people, processes, structure, or the tools they use to manage projects and staff.

Instead, they surmised that acquisitions would be a simple solution. By "writing a check" to buy a firm and "bolt on" the acquired staff, offices, and clients, they assumed the company would grow. The collective knowledge in the room—strong in technical areas, but weak in business matters—had led them down the wrong path.

THE TEAM WITH THE BEST BUSINESS SKILLS WINS

Strategic Goal: Expand the firm's transportation market share

Strategy Driver: Several of the firm's owners were transportation engineers and planners who were well-connected with the regional state agencies. Some had even worked at those agencies.

Ten years before, the firm had engaged a facilitator to help it develop a strategic plan. One goal was to expand market share in transportation by opening offices in several target states. The owners were able to open four new offices and grow staff in each, largely as a result of state government transportation contracts. That is, until the Great Recession came along.

Almost overnight, layoffs reduced staff by 50 percent, a modest profit turned into a loss, and the firm hit its bank borrowing limit. This led to austerity actions and many benefit cuts. Training declined to zero. To finance some senior retirements, the company had to create a 30 percent employee stock ownership plan (ESOP).

The economy eventually recovered and the firm was able to pay down its debt and hire some staff. But profit remained under 5 percent by the time I arrived on the scene.

My solution was to deliver two business learning curricula in advance of strategic planning. First, members of the board of directors and the executive management team were drilled in how to identify which markets and services were most attractive for their business model. We compared these markets and services with the plan they had implemented and refined it accordingly.

Then, I taught the larger strategic planning team about influence, growth barriers, and methods to transform commodity services into high-value services. The team was now ready to analyze their position and to develop a strategic plan with achievable outcomes.

Selecting One Business Model Paves the Way

One of the critical mistakes of the original plan was a lack of understanding of business models. I teach three fundamental models that reference *The Discipline of Market Leaders* by Michael Treacy and Fred Wiersema: (1) a firm that tries to be all models will struggle; (2) the actions required by each model will conflict with the other models; and (3) it is best to choose one, and excel at that.

For instance, an operational efficiency model generally means advanced degrees are not necessary. The client is not going to pay the rate for these professionals, and the work is mostly viewed as commodity and thus can only be differentiated by price. On the other hand, a firm that pursues a service leadership model is striving to be the best in the business to secure the most complex and creative work. This type of firm hires a lot of professionals with advanced degrees and its salary and billing structure are much higher. Can you see the conflict in trying to do both?

So, back to the story. In this case, the firm did not recognize that it was choosing the transportation market in states where the only business model the client's procurement allowed was the operational efficiency model because selections were price-based. The firm had to keep the cost of its services low while maintaining quality control and a minimum level of customer service. The states where they concentrated their efforts all had onerous contract requirements with overhead caps, salary billing caps, profit caps, and even exclusions of some normal business expenses from allowable overhead calculations. This ate even further into the contract-limited profit.

The firm's employees enjoyed the project work but its clients only selected firms on price. Margins were thin. When the recession hit, the state agencies cut back their infrastructure programs. This reduction of business threw the firm's precarious balance sheet into disarray. The unintended consequences of cutbacks led to a decline in process controls and a stagnation of talent. When the recovery came, the firm did not have the technical talent, the business expertise, or the funds to invest in restoring the firm.

Once I had tutored the company's management team and strategic planning team in business growth fundamentals, they made much better choices during the strategic planning workshop, including more accurate market and services assessments and more cogent and impactful SWOT analyses. The firm also decided to transition to a different model that would reduce its dependence on lower-margin business and evolve its commodity services into higher-margin services by learning and investing in cutting-edge design automation, remote sensing, and big data solutions. The team also learned how to navigate through the big agencies to identify procurements that had more favorable contracting requirements.

NAKED ENTRY CATCHES A COLD

Strategic Goal: Expand into stronger markets

Strategy Driver: The firm's workforce lacked the requisite expertise to win new business in the target area, so it needed to hire key people.

This architecture firm had retained a business consultant to analyze its markets and services and compare them with industry forecasts. The consultant recommended a move into medical facilities and senior housing. The owners acknowledged that the firm's core markets were in decline and that other markets were expected to do well in the current economic cycle. But first, they would need to upgrade their staff.

A central action item of this strategy was to hire industry insiders who would understand their prospects' concerns and know how those prospects buy. Their connections would facilitate interactions that would lead to sales.

After a long search and a 25 percent recruiting firm commission, the firm landed a senior-level person in each industry. After several "get to know us" sessions and a bevy of press releases, the individuals were set loose.

However, it quickly became apparent that while the new hires did know the business, their contacts were fairly limited and most of those contacts were not the decision makers. Also, the new hires had no sales training and simply tried to identify projects rather than qualify leads and develop relationships. They did not have the technical knowledge to talk about solution alternatives with prospects and required a lot of support from senior staff. This pulled staff away from their billable work, causing them to worry about their own project obligations and utilization goals, so they began to resist participating in meetings. "I am too busy" became a common excuse.

Two years later, one of these senior people went back to his industry and the other defected to a competitor that already had market penetration. It turned out that hiring a cadre of outside people to build a new market from scratch was very difficult.

When the firm brought me on to help, I could immediately diagnose the problem. First, there wasn't true buy-in from anyone other than the two owners, so the personnel who were meeting prospective clients didn't really "own" or feel invested in the campaign. Second, the firm did not immediately send the new hires to much-needed sales training. They only knew how to ask about projects and were not skilled in building trust beyond the connections they already had in the industry. Thirdly, they had weak support from the home office. The one marketing person was really a senior administrator who I had worked with at a smaller firm years before. She knew proposals but nothing about designing lead-generation campaigns or coaching the individuals on best actions and positioning.

Fully Understand How to Support a New Effort

Unfortunately, I had seen this phenomenon before. Firms start out with a strategic plan that looks good on paper (hire key people; expand into new markets), but they underestimate the complexity of carrying it out. Unless you've been through it before, it's hard to gauge how challenging it can really be.

For this reason, I operate a business learning program to make sure all participants understand the stages of selling. This covers topics such as contemporary lead generation systems, methods to rate and rank leads to manage costs and increase focus, barriers to entering new markets and cross-selling services, and learning about the level of effort and commitment required to undertake such an initiative.

When we delve into the finer points of business-related topics prior to the strategic planning workshops, I'm always impressed by how the business skills modules I teach have elevated the conversations and analysis. It is precisely that education that empowers participants to produce a powerful, well-constructed, achievable plan.

Without this broad knowledge, the team will work with their current understanding of business. This restrains their ambitions and leads them toward less profound outcomes. Since they don't understand the more complex business causes and effects, they tend to stick with what they know, rather than stretching beyond their current world.

Some leadership teams might recognize this limitation and select an external consultant to provide business guidance during the strategic planning workshop. This conflicts with the truth that those involved with the strategy must be fully vested in the strategies and tactics. If the goals are heavily shaped by a consultant, my perspective is that the required buy-in will be at risk.

I agree it is better to have a business consultant with business knowledge than simply facilitation skills. It is even better if the strategic planning team begins the strategic planning process with uniform understanding of the elements of business growth. This occurs when the business learning is accomplished prior to the strategic planning process.

PACK MORE PUNCH

Earlier we talked about the Good Enough Zone. Running a strategic initiative with a team of people who are skilled in their area of expertise but lack business knowledge keeps you firmly ensconced in that zone—it's good enough to get by, but to really thrive in a competitive industry, it's essential to supplement their skill set with some fundamentals in business management.

Each company has its own unique circumstances and priorities that drive strategy planning. An advanced business learning curriculum should be designed accordingly, but should include as many topics as time and resources permit. By elevating the business acumen of the team, the firm has taken a major step to ensure its strategies will become reality.

It is my experience that when you apply business science to the planning process, your strategy becomes more sophisticated. The tactics become clearer, sharper, and more innovative. The team becomes more versatile and proficient at handling unforeseen challenges. Their backgrounds might be in architecture or engineering or design, but now they understand the connection between their world, which is largely technical, and the world of managing a business. It's a formidable, one-two combination for any firm that strives to be a leader in the industry.

In the next chapter, we'll look at how aligning the goals of staff with the goals of the executives and the organization as a whole ensures that everyone is on board with a strategic plan and fully committed to seeing that plan realized.

CHAPTER 7

WHY DO YOU COME TO WORK?

Any kind of business initiative works best when the employees who carry it out understand there's something in it for them too. That's not being selfish; it's just human nature. Therefore, strategy execution functions best when you can align the company's goals with the goals of individuals. This chapter will teach you how to do that in ways that excite and energize staff and offer them a fresh way of looking at their role within the organization.

If a friend kindly asked you to jump off a bridge, would you? Of course not. If doing so was for some reason in the best interests of the person asking you, would it matter? Of course not. Generally speaking, if something runs counter to your own interests, you're not going to do it.

Now, consider a similar but more relatable scenario. If employees were asked to do something that was contrary to their interests (even if it benefited their employer), would they comply? Perhaps—grudgingly—but they'd probably just do the bare minimum to avoid being chastised (or fired). However, would they buy in? Would they really be on board?

In that case, you just have mere *compliance*. You don't have real cooperation. Strategy execution needs cooperation: active, enthusiastic participation from all members.

Don't Assume Alignment

Owners often automatically assume that employees will go along with any request from management without fully considering the ramifications for employees. CEOs and management teams regularly develop strategies, select goals, and launch process improvements aimed at profoundly affecting the company's future. Many times those initiatives are launched with great fanfare. The CEO confidently announces that the company will be a much better place to work if employees get on board, trumpeting more revenue, more profit, more offices, more services, more markets, and more shareholder value.

But how does the staff really feel? Do they share the executive's exuberance? "I'm glad that the executives have figured out what they want, but it doesn't affect me. There is nothing in that plan for me. In fact, it sounds like a lot of busy work that will take me away from what I really like to do."

This employee reaction is common, and it's one of the foremost reasons that initiatives fail. Most strategies simply do not relate to the employees. When asked to implement strategies that are inconvenient or move them outside of their comfort zone, they are not going to jump on board.

Mike McMeekin, PE, chairman of the board and former president of Lamp, Rynearson & Associates, recalls the evolution of the firm's strategic plans. He offers a valuable lesson about why creating arbitrary benchmarks of progress has little utility when it comes to motivating people:

> "At times we had people on our strategic planning team who were convinced that we needed numeric growth goals for revenue and number of employees. I felt that there was not a basis for the numbers being thrown out to the team. The numeric goals we set were prerecession, and we did not come close to meeting the numeric goals in the time frame in the plan. After the recession, we made the decision to define growth in terms of services, expertise, and reputation."

Over the years I have found that strategic plans whose goals for growth are clearer and more explicit tend to garner broader support in the organization. "Developing expertise" is a universal goal of most professional firm employees. "Reputation," another trait valued by individual employees, goes hand and hand with expertise. Thus, rather than measuring success in broad, impersonal terms of "revenue" or "number of employees," it's important to emphasize qualities that resonate with staff. Meet them at their level.

Many organizations can't get their strategy off the ground because of *disconnected goals*. Strategy fails when owners' goals are disconnected from those who are expected to execute the policy (namely, the firm's employees).

Fred Kramer of Stantec's Building Division puts it this way:

> "The role of leadership is vision, people, guidance, and team building as well as alignment of corporate goals and individuals' goals. Somehow you've got to get those tumblers to fall into place. Leaders create the inspiration

and paint the picture. If you can't paint the picture, you're dead. Especially if you're in a design firm. You've got to motivate people. Find out why this is going to be good for them. Not good for you—good for *them*."

So, *paint the picture.* Even if a strategy addresses valid business initiatives, if it does not converge with employees' goals, it simply isn't going to work.

That said, before developing company strategies, there must be a process in place to first uncover employees' goals.

Employees' passion is intertwined with their personal goals, so your strategy must *begin* with employees' goals and then bring those goals in sync with those of the corporation. If employees see the company making a concerted effort to turn personal goals into corporate goals (and as long as those goals have merit), they will be motivated to carry out the challenging work of strategy execution.

Al Curran learned a valuable lesson about connecting personal goals with corporate goals. He and Frank Woodard, PE, founded Woodard & Curran in 1979 through the acquisition of a fifteen-person office. Over the next thirty years, Curran's and Woodward's leadership achieved an organic growth rate of over 20 percent.

Here, Curran describes the philosophy that led to this tremendous growth:

> "My primary interest was to create an organization where people really enjoyed their work and where people recognized that there were many different career paths. There were folks who would much prefer to jump in their car and go have a cup of coffee with their client before they went to work. And there were others who would much prefer getting to work at 6:30 to dive into the calcula-

tions of a hydraulic model and everything in between. And there were folks who really enjoyed working with people, being team leaders and nurturing others "We recognized that everyone had a need to understand the business of the business, not just the technology of the business. And we supported them to grow personally, so that they themselves could understand fundamentally what their personal strength was and understand whether it was driven by what they had learned in their technical training or whether it was something they had learned through other life experiences."

GIVE YOUR EMPLOYEES ROOM TO GROW—THE FIRM WILL GROW WITH THEM

Having worked with Al Curran for ten-plus years as a firm principal, I was able to observe how this philosophy benefited many, including myself. I joined the firm after working for three engineering firms. Those firms did not know how to empower employees and they weren't adequately emphasizing growth. Woodard & Curran was different.

At first, I chose to work toward ownership. The minimum criteria for ownership included metrics such as new revenue bookings, revenue under management, profit, client satisfaction, and a two-out-of-three shareholder vote. I achieved these in my first eighteen months and was elected a shareholder.

Next, I worked toward being a practice leader. I got involved with regional and national waterworks organizations, joined committees (one of which I chaired for twelve years), and published and presented many times. I became a trainer for utility staff, delivering more than fifty classes. I also tracked the latest technologies and differentiated myself as an expert in the newer groundwater sustainability methods, treatment methods, and control technologies. This expertise supported sales and also facilitated key hires through my professional network. In this way, I became the firm's waterworks practice leader and generated more than $10 million in revenue.

After this, I set my sights on business roles. I became a member of the board of directors' finance committee, and later, the board committee on expansion and strategy execution. I also grew into new positions that were market-focused and led the firm's growth in the municipal market and all of the firm's services applicable to that market. We modified our client approach to focus on the number of services provided per client and we grew that from an average of two services to seven. The revenue per client then leaped by a factor of seven. For several years I was the highest-profit, lowest-cost-of-sales principal, the result of mining relationships with top-quality clients.

Al Curran also collaborated with me on several special projects such as reorganizing the board of directors to include voting external board members, which necessitated rewriting the ownership bylaws, selling the plan to shareholders, and identifying, interviewing, and then securing an election for the new board.

We also worked together to make our first acquisition, a consulting firm that delivered digital control solutions that we identified as a new and high-potential business. And, through a board subcommittee, we implemented a novel approach to solicit business proposals from entre-preneurial employees. Five proposals out of twenty that were submitted were accepted, which led to expanding into new geographies and entering new markets.

Over more than a decade, I was given latitude to pursue my interests and to change them as my perception of my strengths and interests evolved. Compared to my previous positions, this was empowering. The CEOs at my former employers told me to just stick to my role and do it well. I did, for a while—and then left to join a firm that respected my talent and ambition.

DON'T FORCE GOOD LEADERS INTO A SMALL BOX

Allow me to share with you another story of disempow-erment that I witnessed with one of my first employers. My office was next to a senior manager, Seth, who was promoted to shareholder and told to shift his focus to a particular client, a large agency. It was not a move that he favored. He loved applying his expertise and he enjoyed deep relationships with his existing clients. As a project engineer, I had accompanied him to client meetings and saw the respect his clients had for him. He had even been named "Man of the Year" in one of his client communities and his picture was splashed across the front page of the local newspaper. I was impressed by his dedication.

Despite his strong reputation and consummate profes-sionalism, that same year, Seth was terminated because he would not change his focus to this large agency. A year later, his project manager left the firm to work for the client that had recognized Seth. The following year, that client discontinued using the firm as they knew what had happened and they lost respect for the firm.

This was an early lesson about two business truths. First, a diversity of leadership styles is healthy and desirable. Second, ego clouds judgment when it interprets someone else's success as a threat. This leads to harmful behavior.

EVERYONE'S MOTIVATION MUST BE TRANSPARENT

It is so critical for owners to understand and embrace what motivates staff. There is a simple way to do that: ask them!

During many workshops I've conducted over the decades, one of my favorite exercises is to ask staff, "Why do you come to work? Please write down only one reason." I employ an anonymous process, so they know that they can write absolutely anything down without being "outed."

Then I post the answers on a flip chart and consolidate them into categories: Financial Motivation; Social or Peer Motivation; and Engaging Work. At this point, everyone sees that their colleagues have diverse reasons for working at the firm. This sparks a discussion about motivation and willingness to embrace change.

Next, I refer to the flip chart list and ask the group if they would be willing to learn and apply new skills if they knew it would enhance their core motivators. They always say yes. I can tell that they suspect that there's a catch, but as a leader, it's important to demonstrate that there is no catch. This is sincere. It's real.

Now that you have their attention, you can go for the slam dunk by declaring, "For those of you who are motivated by money, the strategies we select over the planning sessions will provide you more of it. For those who enjoy social motivations such as companionship or being mentored, the strategies we select will attract professionals who are compatible with our culture and who will teach you more about your area of interest. Finally, for those of you who are thrilled by interesting work, our strategies will engage your desire to take on challenging, enjoyable, long-term projects. Now, will all of you commit to helping us achieve this?"

I always get a yes. And by asking this publicly, they all see the overt, collective buy-in. Of course, saying it is easy. Now comes the hard part: you have to follow through.

The main reason people don't change is fear. You need to eliminate that fear by converting the negative energy of fear or doubt into positive energy. As Kerry Patterson writes in *Influencer: The Power to Change Anything*, "Make the undesirable desirable."

But how do you accomplish that?

First, you acknowledge that implementing a new strategy requires change, and change will move people out of their comfort zone. But make clear that you are going to reduce their risk of failure by giving them support, such as education, coaching, instruction, and patience. This approach demonstrates that you have confidence in your employees' capabilities.

Ultimately, if you understand employees' goals, promise that the corporate goals will align with their own interests, and show that you will provide support . . . you will cultivate an atmosphere for successful change.

DON'T DICTATE BEHAVIORS, *INFLUENCE* THEM

There are many ways to manage influence, but I practice the following approach (inspired by Kerry Patterson). Let's call items 1–6 "influence elements." Item 7 ties them together.

1. Unleash **personal motivation** by overcoming fears and resistance to change.

2. Give people the **capability to excel** in new areas through learning programs.

3. Create **positive social pressure** by enlisting opinion leader participation.

4. Create **teams that share efforts** so that pride in accomplishments is shared by many.

5. **Provide structure** to hold everyone accountable by applying rewards and consequences.

6. Create a **physical office environment** that makes it comfortable to share and talk about change.

7. Employ every single one of these methods on any change initiative to **over-determine[7] success**.

Define Business Goals to Resonate with Staff

Let's examine how reframing goals can emphasize the synchronicity and symbiosis of corporate and personal interests. The table below provides examples of strategic goals, the business objective, and the

---

7 "Over-determination" describes when a certain outcome is brought about by multiple factors. If one of the tactics is omitted or poorly executed, the outcome will still be realized thanks to the other factor(s).

employees' objective. Consider, for example, column 1a, which references the goal of creating wealth by increasing shareholder value. That could be seen as divergent from employees' goals because the owners' wealth doesn't directly benefit them. They might even see it as contrary to their own interests as profits are steered toward the owners rather than the workers. A win-win goal might be phrased as "Achieve financials that fund all employees' financial goals."

EXAMPLES OF CORPORATE-PERSONAL GOAL ALIGNMENT

#	CORPORATE GOAL	PERCEIVED BY EMPLOYEES AS	PERSONAL GOAL	WIN-WIN GOAL
A	Increase shareholder value	Create wealth for owners	Financial security	Income that funds everyone's retirement
B	Sell the company	Create wealth for owners	Job stability	Secure an owner with a history of stability
C	Sell the company	Create wealth for owners	Enjoy working for their supervisor	Secure an owner whose values and culture align with ours
D	External succession: hire or sale	Lack of confidence and support	Career growth	Gain a fresh leadership perspective
E	Diversify to capitalize on growing markets	Unfamiliar client types may be less fun	Enjoy their projects	Enter markets that provide opportunity for all
F	Diversify to capitalize on higher-demand services	Job threat due to mismatch in skills	Enjoy their projects	Leverage skills and adapt them to new and exciting services
G	Elevate the professionalism of corporate services	More red tape and disruption	Enjoy their environment	Employ best practices that keep the company efficient and strong

Or, as in items b and c, if the owners are considering selling the company, employees almost always feel at risk no matter which of the three work motivations apply. These employees:

- are nervous about their financial future;

- fear they will lose their workplace social environment;

- lament that the mentor who they valued all these years will leave the firm;

- fear they may be relocated somewhere that they don't want to be; or,

- are anxious that the kind of projects that they've enjoyed will no longer be a priority.

Instead of simply describing the goal as "selling the company," restate it as "Secure an owner with a history of stability" or "Secure an owner whose values and culture align with ours." It could be explained that the company is doing this to make changes that will expand employees' career opportunities, such as attracting new talent, delivering new services that are in demand, and improving flexibility to locate people in different, exciting geographic areas. New markets and services can be portrayed as creating the opportunity for employees to work on new and interesting projects.

If a strategy involves hiring a new CEO externally, recognize that employees may feel demoralized about a perceived lack of confidence and support (item d). To avoid this, don't label the effort as "seek an external CEO." Label it as "Gain a fresh leadership perspective" to shift the focus to a desire to stimulate employees' careers.

Critics might allege that this is just "wordsmithing"—a kind of rhetorical trick to hide the goal's true purpose. Trust me, if it were, employees would see right through it. Rather, what I am suggesting is that words and framing do matter, as I've learned time and time again in my experience as a consultant and strategist. Goals described in terms of a common purpose are far more likely to be supported. Stephen Robbins and Timothy Judge, who literally wrote the book on organizational behavior, also emphasize this tactic in *Essentials of Organizational Behavior.*[8]

If the goal is to make the firm more geographically diverse, the higher-level purpose might be revenue continuity. The intention is to insulate the firm from local market swings. To employees, this means being exposed to new project concepts and providing the flexibility to relocate.

If a company decides to invest in key hires, that means new mentoring opportunities will arise for staff, who may also be exposed to pretty cool projects.

A strategy to elevate the business impact and internal influence of corporate services groups could be framed as benefiting all staff. When a firm is small, often individuals have to fill roles that do not align with their core expertise. For example, some of the human resources responsibilities may be undertaken by an administrative assistant. A senior project manager might also fulfill office manager duties part-time along with his/her project responsibilities.

Such people might think that responsibility or prestige are taken away from them when a specialist is hired. Instead, make the point that they will have more time to focus on what they do best. The valid business reason is to enhance the growing firm's capability to manage risk and inefficiencies and to handle more complex operations of a growing firm while keeping everything intact from the employees' perspective.

---

8   Stephen P. Robbins and Timothy A. Judge, *Essentials of Organizational Behavior* (New York: Pearson, 2016).

A company that connects its corporate goals to individual goals has a better chance of succeeding at strategic initiatives. If employees recognize that the employer's concern for their well-being is sincere, if the employer seeks to cultivate an organizational culture in which benefits are shared widely, and if the employees can see that changes and growth can directly serve their own diverse interests, the employees reward the employer with continued commitment to the firm. Owners can use this process to gauge the validity and viability of their planned strategic initiatives. After all, employees are the company's most valuable asset, so their retention is critical no matter what company initiatives are involved.

The last few chapters have served to lay the groundwork for building a stellar strategy. Now that you better understand the kind of foundation an organization must have in place, in Chapter 8, we'll get into the nuts and bolts of strategy development.

STRATEGY DEVELOPMENT

Countless books have been written about business and organizational strategy, but few of them offer practical guidance for executing your strategy. With that in mind, I've written this book to position you for success before you even start developing your strategy.

Meticulous planning and prudent development beget successful execution. Executing strategy is a much bigger and more challenging undertaking than the strategy development process. Therefore, the more you invest in the planning phase, the smoother your implementation phase will be.

WHAT IS STRATEGY?

"Strategy" is a broad term that means different things in different contexts, so let's start with an operable definition. BusinessDictionary.com offers two definitions of "strategy," both of which work for me. First, "a method or plan chosen to bring about a desired future, such as achievement of a goal or a solution to a problem." Second, "the art and science of planning and marshalling resources for their most efficient and effective use."

We use the term strategy when we desire a future that's different from what exists today and we are ready to work toward obtaining that future. It could be a single strategy, such as developing a professional-level sales process, or it could be a set of steps identified in a strategic plan. A strategic plan is a comprehensive set of strategies designed to achieve a certain outcome in accord with the long-term vision of what the company seeks to become, and within a defined timeline, usually five years out.

"Strategies" are differentiated from "tactics," which are the smaller and more detailed activities that advance the goals. Tactics can also be described as the incremental steps, elements, or action items that help achieve the strategy's desired outcome.

Let's say you have the strategic goal of "achieving broad participation to accelerate revenue growth." And that goal might be in support of a long-term vision such as "be a top three provider of environmental services in (a particular geography or market)."

Examples of tactics to achieve that strategy might include identifying sales process choices, reviewing the sales processes to determine which sales process fits, and then arranging for sales training. Such tactics might be deployed in the first year following strategy development. Year Two tactics might be to develop processes to manage sales and to coach those who are involved in ways to apply the new sales skills.

I take the time to talk about strategy versus tactics because I have observed that technical staff is fairly good at thinking tactically, but strategic thinking is often a foreign idea. Thus, one of the opportunities you should emphasize during strategy development is allowing those involved to learn how to think strategically and begin to apply this in their daily job.

An exercise I have found useful in helping staff see the difference between strategy and tactics is to have them create a list of what they need to do to secure their desired future. The list they generate tends to identify actions that can be achieved within a few months or which are very general, rather than those objectives that are likely to be achieved on a longer time frame (within five years).

Then, I ask them to update the list with tactics for Year Two. When they are finished, I instruct them to add tactics for the third year. By now, they start to realize that some tactics they've identified are too general and need to be replaced with more concrete ones. That is okay. When they are done, I ask them what benefit they will have realized when they have finished the Year Three tactics. That benefit will actually be the strategy itself.

THE IMPORTANCE OF DIRECTION

Jack Welch, former CEO of General Electric, famously said of strategy: "Pick the general direction and implement like hell." What did he mean by that? Why didn't he say "Create clear and precise goals and work like hell?" Why did he seem to be okay with advancing toward a general goal instead of concretely specifying an objective or series of objectives? Might this "generality" lead to waste and redo?

Let's go back even further than that. Why pick a direction at all? I think we can agree that in business, in life, in virtually any human pursuit, you need to point yourself in the general orientation of your goal, or you'll just be adrift, aimless, going in circles (or backward). We all know people who go through life without picking a direction.

They always seem to struggle with troubled relationships, low-level jobs (maybe no job at all), no family or friends or community to root them, etc.

Choosing a direction means making firm choices. "Firm" doesn't mean irrevocable—just because you pick a direction doesn't mean you're obligated to remain on that course your entire life. The important thing is that we're moving in the general direction of our goal. Navigational tweaks to straighten our path are just part of the process. So we don't need to overly fret about the precision of that direction.

In a business environment where we work in teams, the direction is a choice made by many. Each person has his or her own priorities and desired style, pace, and personal goals. The "general direction" Welch speaks of is the aggregation of many different personalities and interests, the net product where common ground is revealed. Therefore, it will never be precise. That doesn't matter. What matters is that we "work like hell" toward the goal we have chosen.

TURN THIS BOAT AROUND!

Some years ago, I was retained by a five-office regional A/E firm on a turnaround mission. The company was clearly headed in the wrong direction; in fact, it was in crisis. The recession had shrunk revenue and staff. Many key leaders had left. Desperate, the owners were submitting proposals on every publicly advertised project they could locate. They had two full-time salespeople whose mission was to find as many RFPs as they could. Their sales costs were high. Their hit rate was only 15 percent, and the projects they won were low margin. One hiccup and that margin vaporized and became a loss.

I sat with the beleaguered CEO and laid out a plan for an abrupt change in direction. Given the direness of the situation, he was willing to take a chance on what I proposed. He authorized me to shake things up.

To begin, I laid out an extensive sales training program, not just for revenue-generating staff, but also the operations staff, including the CFO. One quarter of the employees went through a three-day sales-training program. At its conclusion, each person knew the techniques, theory, and tools to be effective at sales. This was a step forward, but was this the strategy? No, it was not. Was this the change in direction? No, it was not.

The dramatic directional change was to stop submitting on publicly advertised RFPs. Immediately. The employees were in shock. They feared for their careers. Several very senior engineers and architects expressed concern directly to me and said, "How will we win work without RFPs?"

But they had no choice but to pursue the new direction. The CEO had decided, correctly, that it was change now or perish. Therefore, the new path was to only pursue clients who valued relationships, were themselves effective managers, and who had demonstrated high integrity. And to do this, the revenue-focused staff had to develop relationships while evaluating prospects' match with these pursue/drop criteria.

A critical element of this strategy's successful execution was that I did not leave staff to fend for themselves. I supported them along the way and showed them there was an alternative to RFPs. I trained some of the employees to be relationship sales coaches and I myself coached teams on the most complex pursuits.

We also established tracking systems for each stage of our selling process (the Revenue Forecasting Tool, or RFT, I discussed in Chapter 3). This simple time sheet system measured the level of effort in each sales stage, from lead, to qualified lead, to relationship efforts, opportunity development, and backlog. The data tracked progress toward the goal of generating new revenue. As staff saw this progress, enthusiasm for the new process grew.

The sales training was one tactic. Creating sales coaches was another, and measuring activity in each sales stage quickly revealed that relationships *were* forming and that opportunities for new business *were* growing in number. A year later, the firm was booking high-margin work. The firm submitted 65 percent fewer proposals but won nearly all of them. Backlog soared and profit shot up. Many celebrations took place in an office whose mood was dismal and desperate not long ago.

Naturally, we had to make adjustments along the way. We learned that not everyone was good at each stage of the sale. Some were good at meeting people, others were comfortable developing relationships, and still others were good at working with prospects on the details of the projects. And yes, there were still RFPs to which we responded, but only if we were prepositioned and knew the outcome was likely to be good.

The bottom line is we set a new direction and worked like hell, making periodic adjustments en route to record firm revenue, profits, and stock price. And together, we savored the pride and satisfaction of accomplishment.

THE POWER OF PERSEVERANCE

It's crucial that the strategic planning component establishes a clear direction toward which all decisions will be oriented. Following Jack Welch's blunt advice helps an organization stay focused and avoid distractions so time and money are productively spent "executing like hell."

In the above example, a number of circumstances could have caused the effort to fail. What if the CEO had backed down and not supported the abrupt change in direction? What if he had been tentative and pushed for an incremental approach? He did endure a lot of pressure from one member of the management team in particular who felt her value would be diminished. But he stuck to it. And I stuck to my plan. As I described in Chapter 4, a strong leader who adheres to a worthy, highly visible, and simple message, and then secures followers with whom that message resonates, will see his or her leadership validated.

At first, the CEO looked like a "lone nut." But later, with the company's valuation at a record high and shareholders' wealth through the roof, the CEO was a hero.

THE STRATEGIC PLANNING CHECKLIST

When it comes to the professional services industry, the following components are particularly important for implementing a successful strategic planning effort.

1. Mission statement

The mission statement is a one- to several-sentence declaration that defines who the company is today. It articulates how your business is different from others, or even unique in the industry.

This statement must (1) explain how your business makes your customers' lives better and/or (2) consider what your business does for employees and/or (3) identify what the business does for its owners. Here are two examples:

Our company is about people—clients, employees, and consultants—and enjoying what we do. We believe a shared passion for success requires our commitment to quality.

XYZ Architects brings a team planning and design approach to Canada's infrastructure and economic development solutions. Our employees combine their analytical and creative skills to fulfill clients' business objectives.

The mission statement is mostly an internal statement that identifies the firm's current values and the impact those values have on the employees and the world right now. It is a baseline to help in planning for the future.

2. Vision statement

The vision statement takes an organization's core values, which may be identified in the mission statement, and considers what the organization would be like if those values were maximally realized. It is important to be aggressive in creating a vision statement because it has both internal and external applications. You will often use it on your website, in proposals, and when communicating to the world about what kind of company you are. Make it bold, profound, and memorable.

Here is an example:

BCD will be the engineering, planning, and science consulting firm most admired for its ability to deliver socially conscious services that directly benefit our clients' core business.

The vision statement goes to the heart of the values of the employees and management team in particular—as well as the markets you serve and the services you provide. It also reflects the firm's persona in terms of social trends, financial issues, and current technologies. The vision statement becomes a guiding light in the development of strategies and their execution.

The words and phrases chosen for the vision statement should guide all strategies and tactical decisions. They provide a framework for what not to do as well as what to do. This serves to keep the firm from deviating from its chosen priorities. For example, for the phrase "most admired," a tactic might be to regularly conduct surveys measuring which firm clients most admire. Then, branding, hiring, public relations, and project outcomes are all targeted to advance this part of the vision.

3. Motivation

What is motivating your desire to develop a strategy or a strategic plan? It could be seeking additional revenue, responding to competitive forces, or solving problems like low profits. Your motivation could also reflect awareness that there are attractive opportunities in the marketplace, such as new markets or changes in the growth of particular markets or services. Your services may have evolved with the introduction of new technologies and other innovations, and this could be a factor as well. Ownership challenges could be another motivator for strategy development. Perhaps a company desires more owners as part of its sustainability campaign. Similarly, ownership issues could also involve succession planning—not just in terms of ownership, but in terms of any key positions within the firm as well.

Any of these issues could provide motivation for developing a strategic plan. It is important to have discussions in advance of strategic planning to understand these motivating factors, both overt (publicly safe) and covert (goals people prefer not to reveal publicly because they are self-serving or expose weaknesses or fears).

4. SWOT analysis

SWOT stands for "strengths, weaknesses, opportunities, and threats" and is a core part of any strategic planning effort. It will help you generate a list of goals, strategies, and action items/tactics.

The SWOT process allows the firm to recognize and, later in the process, to leverage its most unique strengths and seize on available opportunities. It also examines weaknesses in the company, which could be weaknesses in terms of structure, people, or processes. Generally, it does not concern weaknesses in terms of a particular service area. SWOT weaknesses are broader kinds of weaknesses.

Opportunities often exist outside the company, such as moving into some newer areas. Threats are often external, but not always. Threats can revolve around competitors, changing buying habits, new business models springing up in an ever-changing economy, or other factors.

5. Goals

We often use the acronym SMART to describe the kind of goals for which we want to aim: Specific, Measurable, Achievable, Results-focused, and Time-bound. Once a list of possible strategic goals is generated, they must be consolidated into a manageable few. I like to limit my clients to no more than five goals. A longer list can become unwieldy. It's more effective to have a small set of goals to work toward or your efforts and resources will be spread too thin.

Each of the goals should be accompanied by key performance indicators that measure progress toward each goal, such as comparing against current conditions that might be revealed by the SWOT analysis.

6. Action plan

The action plan contains the to-dos that build toward each goal. To-dos are also the tactics you will pursue to achieve your strategic goals. The action plan identifies what each tactic is, who will lead or be responsible and accountable for each one, and when it is expected to be completed. In this way, you clarify where that tactic falls in the sequence of all the other tactics that support the goal.

It's prudent to pull together the various strategies and strategic plans that your company has created and then evaluate where progress has been made and where barriers exist. In my experience, only 5 percent of plans lead to profound results and only 30 percent lead to any progress at all. Therefore, it's important to understand fully what has and hasn't worked in the past.

It's also important to use this seven-item planning rubric to examine how things have been managed in the past. In previous strategic undertakings, were the strengths and opportunities fully considered alongside the weaknesses and threats? Were the goals articulated clearly? How many of the goals were realized? Retrospectively scrutinizing previous campaigns will sharpen your strategic awareness and hone your planning skills for the current initiative to help ensure that your strategy is realized.

Picking a direction and "implementing like hell" brings about change, and change is always a tricky thing for individuals and organizations alike. Chapter 9 examines how to engage transitional periods head-on and take advantage of the opportunities they present.

CHAPTER 9

TRANSITIONS: GROWING PAINS AND PLEASURES

Transitions present both opportunities and threats. How you respond to them is up to you. You cannot totally *control* your destiny, but you can influence it. If you are among the few who hope your long-term strategies will produce a major transition, this chapter is for you. If you are contemplating the prospect of taking a more aggressive approach to create the future you want, then this chapter is also for you. It will show you what is required. Then you can decide which option serves you best.

In my observation, most professionals don't seek profound change. Profound change is really hard. Profound change requires an enormous commitment to achieve. And the risks of failure are great.

Most of us prefer to stick to our technical interests rather than transform into a serial entrepreneur, which introduces extra risks. But for the successful few who make the transition, the rewards can be immense.

Serial entrepreneurs have obliterated long-held traditions as they've reinvented entire industries. This is how Uber disrupted the taxi industry. This is why the recording industry has been replaced by the music streaming industry. And this is why the traditional professional services industry is about to give way to software firms and progressive manufacturers. Did that statement get your attention?

I present three possible approaches to handling transitions: (1) creating a change culture, (2) top-down ownership of initiatives, and (3) creating win-wins for all employees by emphasizing the fact that change brings fresh opportunities.

THE ANATOMY OF CHANGE

Woodard & Curran had 130 employees and three offices. The firm had always sought growth. It pursued growth, not only for financial gain, but also to create career opportunities for all employees.

Our annual growth goal consisted of dual objectives. One was a base goal of 10 percent revenue growth, which we felt would be sufficient to provide the desired career opportunities. Then there was the stretch goal, which pushed all of the division managers who contributed to the annual business plan to create more aggressive goals to achieve substantial, not just incremental, progress. The outcome was ten consecutive years of 20–30 percent predominantly organic annual growth until we reached five hundred employees.

And what would drive this growth? The creation of a change culture.

The concept was simple—as the lesson of "The Dancing Man" reminds us, having a simple objective is important for starting a movement. At many management meetings we heard the same statement over and over again, hundreds of times: "To remain relevant in the firm as it grows, you must be prepared for the next level."

We knew that growth meant change. Growth creates change. Change in management's business skills was most important, followed by change to the processes used to conduct business, the structure of the firm, and the tools to create efficiency. To achieve 20–30 percent growth, everyone needed to anticipate and be prepared for change. Constantly.

How did we do this? First, we hired persons whose career aspirations made them more open to change. Second, we created a learning program. A two-day annual retreat was organized to prepare us for every aspect of change. One full day was spent on operations (internal matters) and one full day on clients and services (external matters).

Many business consultants delivered one-hour to half-day seminars on team building, leadership skills, management skills, cross selling, sales, cross staffing, interviewing, supervising, motivating, negotiating, account analysis, ownership models, and ethics.

In addition to the annual retreats, senior management was exposed to additional learning programs on topics related to change. For instance, structural changes, large account management, and project management were addressed. Many of the principals also engaged in week-long programs on leadership and managing influence.

In addition to learning programs, we overhauled the board of directors once we hit three hundred employees. We modified the shareholder agreement to allow external board members. Four new members joined the board.

We then established four board subcommittees, each staffed with an external director, an internal director, and shareholders. The learning continued in the form of mentoring from the external directors, including a retired CFO from CH2MHill, the CEO of a top ten ENR firm Roy F. Weston, with whom I had worked in the past, as well as a nationally recognized environmental attorney from Pfizer.

Meanwhile, we changed our approach to meetings. In my experience, most management meetings consist of meandering down lists of actions items, without really involving the group as a whole or tapping into the talent in the room.

This is a poor way to develop an organizational culture that is dynamic, forward-thinking, and growth-oriented. The best kind of meetings are those in which the group shares and solves challenges, and where decisions are made not by the loudest voice, or by the senior-most person in the room, or even by democratic vote, but by *consensus*.

Many staff went through facilitation training so they could learn how to use consensus to make decisions about which actions to take. This meant learning the skills of active listening and responding. Equal contributions, not just from the extroverts, but from everyone. And working toward solutions with which everyone was comfortable.

As a result, participants were focused on collective victory—everyone winning as a group. Dialogue and debate were free, lively, and encouraged. It was competitive, but friendly. This created a change culture based on open dialogue and consensus management.

To be sure, this effort was very expensive. Our profits hovered around 6 percent, well below the industry average due to the investment cost of growth. But share prices leaped 20 percent a year, and in the long run, the tremendous growth justified the cost.

"Change culture" can take many forms, and each organization will take a different approach. I share one that worked, based on emphasizing business learning for a significant number of employees; hiring external business professionals to supplement our technical backgrounds; bringing in external members to the board of directors to deepen the firm's business expertise; and conducting frequent management meetings using consensus techniques to engage all of the participants.

TOP-DOWN LEADERSHIP

Most strategic plans will involve a robust action plan. How proficient is the team who is working to advance each action? We know they are all smart people, but almost always they are, at best, "part-time business professionals." They spend most of their day delivering their technical services to clients.

For major strategic objectives, they require lots of support. Therefore, for the most complex actions, it is often best for the C-suite and senior management, working with external advisors, to take those on. When it comes to objectives like entering new markets, transitioning commodity services to value-add services, or transitioning sales to make full use of digital tools, the pursuit of these goals often stalls without top-level support.

CALLING IN REINFORCEMENTS

The strategic planning team was generally aware of the impact of technology on clients' buying habits and sales solutions, yet no one was an expert on the topic. In the second year of executing the strategic plan, progress on several goals had stalled. The teams working on them had focused on tactics with which they were familiar; however, those concerns that were foreign to them had not advanced.

The marketing department was headed by a talented director, but that department mostly just produced proposals, coordinated trade shows, and periodically updated the firm's website. The director had not been exposed to the new way of selling, which involved a lead-generation focus using detailed inventory of targeted prospects, multilevel outbound marketing solutions such as email campaigns, and inbound solutions using webinars, social media, search engine optimization, and an active blog.

This was too much for the marketing department, which was understaffed and ill-equipped to build such a program. This is where the CEO, CFO, and COO stepped in to lead the charge. They retained a marketing con-sultant who understood the digital solutions, and they outsourced most of the time-intensive list-building and copywriting functions. The marketing director began with a steep learning curve, but she was supported by her superiors.

In this case, the difficult challenge of transitioning the firm's marketing and sales to the new digital age would not have been achieved if the C-suite team had not taken responsibility for making it happen. They were able to see that the teams were struggling with the transition and made a firm decision to outsource the task.

WIN-WIN: EMPHASIZING CAREER OPPORTUNITIES

Many of the growth areas that are impacted by strategic planning will present career advancement opportunities for personnel within the firm. Of course this is encouraged and should be openly discussed to make personnel aware of how strategically planned transitions create the chance to do something new, enriching, and personally beneficial.

The importance of promoting transitions as a career opportunity can't be overstated. You will benefit if valuable employees know that you respect them and want them to remain with the company.

As a company grows, the skills of those in management or leadership roles have to become more robust. This means those people will need to learn and evolve. The SWOT analysis is a useful place to make this clear. During the SWOT analysis, staff begins to envision the future company and they will consider how that future meshes with their personal goals.

This approach isn't necessarily a component of the strategy plan itself, but it is an important consideration when working to build support among staff for the company's imminent transformation. Once it comes time to implement the strategy, it's useful to have the various initiatives that comprise the plan spearheaded by people who are sincerely passionate and have bought into that process. You do not want to have people involuntarily assigned to those roles because without enthusiastic buy-in, those initiatives are less likely to advance.

Respecting Personal Choices

Every employee in the firm is important and valuable, and it's smart to take advantage of upcoming strategy development or strategic planning exercises to let them know this. This is also where you can assure staff that the plan will respect individuals' priorities while simultaneously strengthening the organization. Also make it known that if someone wants to have a different role, maybe one that is less rigorous and involves fewer responsibilities, that's perfectly fine. The firm has a place for them too. These strategies should defuse resistance among people who worry about whether their jobs are safe.

I just completed a strategic plan for a northeast US environmental firm. The firm had recently ventured into new markets, and it wanted to expand services to other geographies and deepen the vertical service groups. As the workshops progressed, one of the participants, Ben, who managed the firm's public sector group, sensed a disconnect between his goals and where the company was heading. He had stepped up years before to lead that group when all their offices were located in his state. Now, after the company had expanded, he could tell that the company's goals were starting to reflect those of a larger multistate firm with national aspirations.

Ben sensed that this new direction was likely to interfere with his personal goals. He began to worry about his job security, how this transition would affect his home life, and how it would impact his client relationships in the territory he had worked in for so long. He began to accept that he might need to make difficult choices.

When strategy is developed, there is always some change. For some employees, change will be perceived as a threat. The threats create negative energy and stall initiatives. Threats are barriers, and they need to be resolved in an open and honest way—and early in the process.

Others see change for the opportunities it offers. Those opportunities can energize a strategic initiative by making employees eager to participate.

Ben talked about his concerns with his superiors and spoke frankly about his career goals and where he wanted to be as part of the execution element of the plan. At the end of those discussions, he was comfortable admitting that he'd rather not be responsible for a larger geographic area and a much larger list of services. His managers recognized Ben's value to the company and wanted him to remain content. They accepted that he wanted to stay closer to home. This is not unusual in the consulting world, and firms should be prepared to address this issue.

In the end, Ben's job description was modified and he moved into another role that was less senior but aligned more closely with his personal goals. It was done with respect and support, and when he was ready to retire from the firm, he was able to look back on his career with the company with pride and satisfaction.

Compare this to other firms that penalize individuals who express reluctance about stepping up, taking on more responsibility, or getting involved with more complex management activities, or individuals who would rather stay closer to the technical center. Many firms would chastise (if not terminate) these people.

This is unfair and imprudent because many of these employees likely have substantial connections within the firm, client relationships, mentoring relationships, and a solid history as contributors to the company.

In other words, that kind of inflexibility is a terrible business practice. Forcing a square peg into a round hole is simply a bad idea. Successful firms frame strategy development and strategic planning as fostering transitions that provide opportunities for advancement.

Honing Your SWOT Thinking

Part of strategic planning involves examining strengths, weaknesses, opportunities, and threats. While the classic SWOT analysis assesses company-level factors, staff will invariably begin to think anew about their roles and how the future might impact them. Thus, the SWOT becomes personalized.

Those who do want to transition into a more senior, complex, or responsible role should be asked to consider what they would need to accomplish that advancement. To start thinking about whether, for instance, they might need a new direct report to help them move into this area. Or, might they benefit from business training and the support of a career coach?

I've always found it helpful to learn by studying the practices of managers of other firms that excel in their field—firms that are larger, more sophisticated, more innovative, or that boast more diverse services or locations. In an article I published in *Industrial Management*,[9] I proposed a method for executives to compare themselves with peers at those next-level firms. Using sources such as LinkedIn, proposal résumés, companies' websites, or direct conversations (usually at a trade show or client comment), senior managers can closely examine the qualities of their counterparts and compare those qualities with themselves. What is different? Where do I match them? Where do they surpass me? How can I further develop my professional attributes to reach their level of success?

When my two hundred–person A/E firm was acquired by a two thousand–person firm, I researched my counterpart at that firm— which was much more powerful in terms of its national presence, the

---

9   Doug Reed, "SWOT Your Way to the Future," *Industrial Management*, March/
     April 2013, 23–26.

size of the team, and a much larger clientele. I could see that for me to advance to that level, I would need to also grow my own career.

This kind of comparative self-assessment is a terrific exercise for a firm that seeks rapid growth. I have asked the senior management team of my clients, "Have any of you managed a unit of a company the size of which you are projecting to be?" Usually the answer was no. So, I would ask, "Once you grow to that size, are you still going to be qualified for a senior management role? If you want to be, you had better improve yourself so that you're on par with the people who hold your same position in the kind of large, prestigious company that you're trying to develop here."

This always generates a lot of discussion. It's a hard truth, but it's the truth. And this personal SWOT analysis will reveal certain realities that compel executives to take a hard look at how their personal goals dovetail with the execution of the organization's strategy.

KEEP IT PERSONAL

Change is scary—but it doesn't need to be. Executives should remain the guiding hand that keeps people on track and reassures them that transitions bring many good things. For one, creating a change culture helps ease the process. Strong, decisive leadership and lending support where support is needed—even if that means expending certain resources or bringing outside experts in to help—is also essential. In addition, keeping the firm and the individuals who comprise it in sync will ensure that people see the transition as a win-win.

Just as the firm's leaders offer support to the people they lead, the executives can also benefit from support themselves. Chapter 10 goes deeper into the subject of "supported execution" and the value of having someone in your corner to fight for you from beginning to end.

CHAPTER 10

SUPPORTED EXECUTION: MANAGING TACTICAL TEAMS

When firms don't seek expert counsel to help them prepare for and then deliver execution, they jeopardize the whole strategy. This chapter explains the importance of having a business professional guide you step by step. It provides a checklist for how to manage the different tactical teams charged with implementing the plan.

Have you ever undertaken a design project where the owners decided to administer the construction without any of your support? It's less than ideal and can be perilous to your firm and the project team. For one, the clients often don't fully appreciate the complexity of construction. They may not even be skilled at operating the built facility.

Fortunately, the standard in our industry is for the designer to remain involved during the construction phase. Some clients do have the capacity to support construction, but even they know it is too risky to completely go it alone.

So what about strategic planning? Isn't executing strategies the hard part, just as construction is the harder part of bringing a new facility online? Isn't it likely that the strategic planning process requires skills that your employees don't possess? It's a wonder, then, that so many firms try to do it all by themselves.

Here is what Mike McMeekin of Lamp, Rynearson has to say about his past experience with strategy execution:

> "A common excuse for delays or failures is that day-to-day work gets in the way. When you assign tactics to busy project staff, the strategic plan duties can be given a lower priority. Another obstacle to success has been poorly thought–out tactics and action items. For us, the formulation of tactics has sometimes taken place outside of the strategic planning workshops without the advice of senior leaders or our consultants. We have learned that senior leaders need to stay involved in tactical execution to ensure that our overall goals receive the strategic thinking they need and deserve."

What Mike has experienced is that members of the firm who are accountable for executing the strategic goals often lack the skills to accomplish the task. They may be terrific managers, but they don't possess the business knowledge to advance the goal. And when everybody is busy delivering services to clients, the implementation of the strategic plan stalls. And we all know that stalled execution can be disastrous.

A FIFTEEN-POINT PLAN FOR SUCCESSFUL EXECUTION

The following checklist is your navigation plan for executing smoothly and efficiently—aided by the support of an outside expert:

1. **Understand and commit to supporting the strategy over the long term, well after it has been defined.** When I first meet with a client, we talk about core drivers and the level of support we can expect. Usually, strategy execution necessitates coaching, facilitation, team engagement, recruiting volunteers, information exchange, meeting minutes, progress reports, external instructors, mentoring, and troubleshooting to work through barriers. I ask clients if they are ready and able to handle this. The expenses too? The nonbillable time that will be spent?

2. **Choose a planning team based on their influence qualities.** Conduct one-on-one conversations with each participant about their level of interest and how they might participate. Make clear that one important role for participants will be persuading those around them to get on board. Also, make sure your planning team understands that they are also responsible for supporting the implementation team in identifying critical barriers that might not be easily visible.

   For this task, I make sure the CEO is clear on the conversation he/she will have with the prospective members of the planning team. Often I call three to six participants myself to gain additional insight on their level of commitment and their past experience with similar strategy initiatives.

3. **Communicate to all employees the firm's long-term goals.** Couch your message in terms of the benefits to individuals within the firm, and not just how it will add value to the company or its owners. Make it about each employee's career while acknowledging the varied interests and priorities of employees.

For this task, I usually provide the CEO with an email template that I've honed over the years to communicate this message effectively. I want to make sure the employees understand the importance of the initiative and know it serves their best interest.

4. **Assess the business acumen of the strategic planning team, both collectively and individually.** It is not adequate if only a few members of the team possess business growth skills. It's essential that *most* of them possess these skills for the overall brainstorming assessment and the alternatives screening process to function well. The more team members who have business knowledge, the more effectively the goals will be executed and the more likely the group is to stay focused.

The CEO and the management team often have a good idea of the business skill of their underlings, and so, at their direction, I often conduct audio or video calls myself with strategy team members to gauge their abilities and see if they have any past experience with strategy development.

5. **Implement a business learning program.** Ideally, this is a long-term program that's both incremental and consistent. If that is not feasible, the program is typically conducted as a pre-strategic planning workshop. It's a good idea to prep participants in advance by assigning "homework" based on useful educational material such as texts, webinars and conference topics, and market/service research.

My program is usually a one-day workshop. There is preliminary work, such as reading articles or reviewing financials. I have a number of curricula from which to choose, depending on the business knowledge of the team and the core drivers of the strategic planning. Some of these programs are described in Chapter 6.

If clients express concern about their processes, I have them complete an online business process assessment survey, and sometimes I have them conduct an employee satisfaction survey if the company has not done so in the last two years. These measures enhance the strategic planning team's understanding of the data and drivers of the strategic planning workshop.

6. **Conduct strategic planning workshops off-site, in a comfortable environment.** These workshops are one to two days in duration and employ a variety of adult learning methods and group facilitation techniques. During the workshop, business analysis methods are taught and applied, and the team consolidates and prioritizes their preliminary goals until they come up with the final three to

five strategic goals and corresponding tactics. The elements of the strategic plan are described in Chapter 8.

My approach to these workshops is multistep. First, as part of the business learning workshop we also learn about classic strategic planning methods. We talk about how to develop a mission statement, vision statement, SWOT analysis, market analysis, and service analysis, and then generate a first pass.

The second step is referred to as "socializing." Members of the workshop take the analysis materials and invite other employees to participate over the following month or two. To socialize the material involves conducting a series of short informal gatherings to share the concepts, hear additional perspectives, and fully develop the material. Interdivision and interdepartmental engagement is encouraged so that common synergies and goals are revealed.

This socializing activity will engage a broader cross-section of participants and encourages partnerships and collaboration. This is important because executing the strategy will require many more staff members to be involved. The more employees who think they have contributed, the stronger the sense of ownership of the outcome.

The results of the socializing events are brought to the final workshop as a starting point to further the analysis, validate conclusions, test ideas, consolidate goals, and specify tactics associated with the final goals. At this point, the strategies are in near-final form.

7. **Between workshops, have corporate support groups such as marketing, finance, IT, HR, and administrative participate in as many socializing meetings as they can.** After all, their mission is to support and lead all units of the company on matters that pertain to their area of expertise. They are also in a good position to spot cross-division synergies and opportunities for multiple groups to combine efforts to advance their common goals.

8. **Immediately after the strategic goals are finalized and an action plan is drafted, deliver a detailed compilation of workshop materials to participants.** Teams are formed around each goal, and volunteers are recruited to advance the goals. Teams will use an action item planning tool, which is simply a table for recording the goal, a statement of the goal's importance, the list of tactics to support the goal, the measurable outcomes of each tactic, and the person who will lead each tactic.

If possible, schedule the first meetings face to face as the groups need time to bond before they can begin working on the goal. Set expectations for meetings, which are typically held monthly. Often, at the beginning, enthusiasm is high and teams may want to meet every other week, which is okay. But expect that fast pace to slow down and for the planning team to revert to monthly meetings. Sometimes groups will end up meeting every two months, particularly during vacation season. Don't worry about this decline as long as they maintain a schedule, there is high participation in their meetings, and people come to the meetings prepared.

9.   **Anticipate that the execution teams will work through the normal "forming, norming, and storming" phases.** The notion of "forming, norming, and storming" was coined in 1965 by group dynamic theorist Bruce Tuckman. When groups first meet, they are "forming": getting to know one another, establishing the dynamics of the group, and clarifying their missions and tactics. They begin "norming" as they achieve clarity on the goals and challenges and start to arrive at a consensus. The real work and progress don't occur until they have reached the "storming phase." Thus, firm leaders should expect at least three meetings to occur before the tactics begin to advance. Firm leaders should also expect that action plans will evolve and priorities will be rearranged as the team process progresses.

Expect that some of the teams will require external training and that some of the tactics will require company-wide training.

My role at each of the strategy execution team meetings is to accelerate this process and to reach the "storming phase" as soon as possible. There can be substantial debate around a group's strategic goal: what it means, why it is important, what tactics are appropriate, who will take the lead, what external support or funds are required, and in what sequence tactics should be accomplished.

This is where an outside business professional—one who understands the business and where it is heading—can help the team. An external facilitator will help maintain momentum, hold the team accountable for meeting and making progress, prevent the team from veering off on tangents, and keep them focused on productive activities that work toward the goal.

10. **Goals are more likely to advance if efforts are led by a volunteer.** Don't "draft" somebody into the position because if they aren't enthusiastic and committed to the goal, they will likely flounder. Focus on tactics that are spearheaded by a single volunteer and advance those goals, setting other goals aside or outsourcing them to external business consultants.

Many times, I have seen tactics stall when individuals were too intimidated to "volunteer." Usually it was because they were not fully committed to the task. I have also witnessed the "I can do everything" person who takes on too much. For instance, in one case, the COO volunteered to lead advancement of the goal. It became clear he was already spread too thin, and we had to find a replacement volunteer. For this reason, it is important to make sure the leader is fully up to the task.

11. **Each of the tactics assigned to each strategic goal should have a scope, schedule, and budget.** Teams are generally familiar with this approach because it's similar to project planning. This is where an external facilitator can support the team by providing clarity on the level of work involved, particularly if it involves developing new processes, assessing markets and services, or learning new skills, such as sales.

Often, at the early stage of the process, teams must determine what external resources are required and what that will cost. These expenses usually require the approval of senior management. It's unlikely that the company will be able to approve budgetary requests for every tactical initiative. The cost will be too high and there may be too much disruption to the staff's normal utilization. So during this "forming and norming" phase, the goal teams will need guidance about how to set priorities that fit within an overall corporate budget. This is usually my role—to help them set those priorities.

12. **Incorporate tactics into the firm's annual business plan.** The individuals responsible for developing an annual business plan should be familiar with each strategic goal. The business plan must explicitly demonstrate that it is aligned with the goals and tactics of each of the goal teams. This prevents conflicts, ensures fluidity and cohesion among different units of the firm, and reinforces the notion that the tactics require the blessing of senior management.

13. **Conduct formal quarterly reviews to examine metrics, validate progress, and resolve barriers.** Don't be concerned if all of the goals aren't advancing uniformly. Each group will be comprised of individuals with varying abilities and the goals and the tactics will have different priorities. Sequencing of goals is acceptable, but make sure that participation remains high and the group is aligned

and feeling good about what they're doing. Avoid applying so much pressure that individuals get burned out.

14. **Recognize individual contributors, but celebrate progress with the whole company.** Remember that this effort is for the benefit of all employees, not just the employees who are directly involved. In pursuit of strategic goals, corporate interests and individual desires must be aligned. Celebrations are an opportunity to reinforce this fact. It's a great idea to publicly share examples or stories with the entire staff about progress. A good way to do this is to conduct a company-wide video conference meeting.

15. **Plan to repeat this process every three to five years.** Maintain focus on advancing the goals over the entire period. After all, each of the tactics is a small step toward the finish line. Advancing tactics is the more concrete, more tangible part of the process and that will end up being what employees remember, enjoy, and learn from the most.

TRUST YOUR TEAMS—BUT SUPPORT THEM WHEN THEY NEED IT

In the twenty-plus years that I've been consulting with professional services firms, I've learned to follow the lead of each goal team. If strategic planning is conducted properly, there will be a high level of enthusiasm and employees will want to advance the goals immediately and not defer them for six months or a year. I prefer to allow all groups to move forward as quickly as they can, and if they run into barriers or find their abilities are stretched to the limit, we can then sequence them. They also may need to pause while some external training is conducted, so it's okay if, over time, only one or two goals advance concurrently.

Meanwhile, ensure that strategy execution is an explicit priority of the board of directors, the CEO, and the management team. If there is not absolute commitment at each of these levels, then progress will stall. I've seen this numerous times.

For example, I've encountered situations where a CEO will lead their company through the strategic planning process, but when it's time for execution, they're intimidated by the effort required, and they dial it back to the point where all momentum is lost. This causes great disillusionment among the team's project managers, division managers, and principals, who complain that the CEO is no longer committed.

The CEO should know in advance that such a move will damage his or her credibility. The CEO must remain committed. Making this a board-level priority will help keep pressure on the management team and the CEO to advance the strategies.

I also sometimes recommend creating a new subcommittee within the board of directors. It could be a strategic plan implementation committee, for instance, and liaisons can be assigned between that committee and the goal groups. This is an excellent way to maintain focus and keep things advancing.

Following the guidelines described in this chapter will leave you well-prepared for the daunting task of execution. Even still, you may be hesitant about strategically transforming your company. The next chapter will assuage your doubts by looking at some common objections to taking the leap that all firms must eventually take to keep growing in a competitive, dynamic industry.

CHAPTER 11

OVERCOME NAYSAYERS AND LAUNCH!

Many professionals provide strategic planning services. Some may seem to have sparkling résumés, a string of fancy titles after their name, and LinkedIn profiles adorned with glowing praise from colleagues. But appearances can be deceiving, and résumés and LinkedIn pages are curated to project a certain image. How do you *really* know if a strategic planning consultant is worth his or her salt?

I recommend you ask prospective consultants this simple question: "How many of your clients have achieved profound outcomes?" Since strategic consultants are normally focused on strategy *development*, they usually don't remain involved in execution, which is when the plan is really tested.

According to a survey I've conducted, only 5 percent of firms have realized profound benefits and fewer than 30 percent receive any significant benefit at all from their strategic-planning investment. And that's assuming the survey respondents answered honestly—we know that people hate to admit failure. I think this occurs because they blame themselves, not the facilitator. After all, he or she was not around for the execution of the strategy. It was not his or her responsibility . . . or was it?

If you're operating a firm that's about to embark on a strategic initiative, your biggest worry is that you'll end up like the 95 percent of your competitors that failed. You want to be among the 5 percent that have been wildly successful.

Here is what it will be like if you follow the guidance provided in this book.

Imagine your staff making the time to participate, to listen to and comprehend your vision, and to help you understand what's really happening at ground level. Picture your people working together to implement initiatives because each person sees how the initiatives support their personal goals. Picture a cohesive, smoothly running workforce that attends to their daily technical and creative responsibilities while simultaneously advancing the broader, organization-wide strategy that you've meticulously designed.

This is what distinguishes stagnant companies from the dynamic, visionary firms that will become the future leaders of the industry.

DON'T MAKE EXCUSES

Naturally, change is scary, and there are always doubts that will hold you back. But not acting—remaining stagnant—is an even scarier and more dangerous proposition.

Let's address some common excuses for avoiding strategy development.

1. "We don't have time."

You know what they say about time: it's the one resource you can't create more of or get back once it's spent. We're all short on it. But ultimately, we choose how we spend our time. If you don't have time, you have to *make* time.

Fortunately, if you hire the right expert, they'll do the heavy lifting for you, so you can concentrate on other things. In addition, a successful strategy often pays dividends in not only capital but also time, creating a more efficient workforce and resolving entrenched problems, allowing you to concentrate on the most productive aspects of your business.

2. "We can do this ourselves."

Yes, you could, in theory, do this yourself. You could also give yourself marriage counseling or perform simple surgical procedures on yourself. But would that be a good idea? Ask yourself this: Do you know of any firms that *haven't* brought in an outside strategic planning expert and have enjoyed resounding success?

Strategic planning is like any other highly specialized skill: it requires an expert to do it right. And not just any expert, but an expert with a wealth of experience in your industry. Moreover, hiring an expert provides an advantage that you don't get from doing it in-house: they'll bring a fresh, outsider's perspective and will take a good hard look at your firm from the outside in as well as the inside out.

3. "It is too expensive."

It's true that it can be costly. But view it as an investment: a good strategy will pay for itself. I'll explain all the costs you should expect.

I'll even introduce you to CEOs who have made the investment so that you can hear their stories directly.

4. "I cannot get full commitment from our staff."

If you try to impose your will in a top-down fashion, you won't. But if the strategy resonates with staff's personal goals and concerns, they will embrace the plan. As we looked at in the book, one of the cornerstones of my approach is encouraging staff buy-in by aligning corporate and individual goals in a win-win fashion.

5. "We have the wrong people in leadership roles."

A good facilitator will help you identify your best influencers and help you bring the right people onto the strategic planning team. If the current leaders aren't up to the job, there are ways to find talented individuals who can step up— people who will not only advance the strategic initiative but could emerge as lifelong leaders within the organization.

6. "Strategic planning goals are often unobtainable."

If you seek to turn your five-person firm into a six hundred–person juggernaut overnight, that won't work. Strategic planning is not miracle work. But the right facilitator who understands your world can help you articulate feasible goals that take advantage of the talent you already have. That's also why we break strategic planning into a series of precisely defined goals and actionable tactics.

7. "Strategic planning will divert my team's attention away from their core job."

Strategic planning is not just about deciding what to do; it's also about determining what to stop doing or to avoid. The strategic approach presented in this book allows staff to contribute to strategy execution without interfering with their day-to-day responsibilities. In fact, my approach has the added benefit of teaching technical personnel valuable business skills that will make them well-rounded, multitalented assets to your firm.

8. "Change is difficult."

If what you're doing is working flawlessly, here's my advice: keep doing it. But if you can identify ways in which your company can improve, then change is imperative. Remember: all good organizations must grow, in one form or another. If you're not growing, you're dying. Change is what powers growth, and growth is how you rise to the top. If you don't do it, your competitors surely will.

NOW THAT YOU HAVE READ THIS BOOK, WHAT IS THAT ONE THING YOU MUST REMEMBER?

Understand that you don't know what you don't know. Set ego aside. Acknowledge that managing a business is very different from managing a project. Sure, we technical people love to solve a challenge, and our first impulse is to work through it ourselves. But when it comes to long-term organizational strategy, this is not the best approach. Expert support is necessary.

If you are an architect, you know not to put your stamp on an engineering drawing. If you are an engineer, you know not to put your stamp on the architectural drawings. And if you are a lab technician or an environmental licensed professional, you are not going to sign off on anything for which you are not certified.

So don't shortchange your business. Seek advice from those with the expertise. Learn, be coached, and develop great strategy. Remember that the road to successful execution is paved far in advance of starting the plan, and don't let up during the execution itself until you are celebrating your and your team's success.

Be one of the 5 percent.

ABOUT THE AUTHOR

As a business consultant and corporate adviser, Doug Reed's passion is showing professional services firm executives how to achieve sustainable growth without compromising vision or integrity. He has worked in the architecture, engineering and environmental fields for over thirty years, many of them spent as an owner of high-growth enterprises. As president of FosterGrowth, he provides management consulting, business learning, strategic planning and strategy execution services to a wide range of companies. Previously, he worked as an engineering executive and was an elected shareholder twice, for an engineering/environmental firm and later for an architecture/engineering firm.

Doug holds a BS and MS in civil engineering and maintains his PE license in several states. He has three children and enjoys music, golf, skiing, and sailing.

www.fostergrowth.biz

dreed@fostergrowth.biz

@fostergrowth

CPSIA information can be obtained
at www.ICGtesting.com
Printed in the USA
FSHW011844130719
59995FS